SAWBILL

SAWBILL

A Search for Place

JENNIFER CASE

University of New Mexico Press ❧ Albuquerque

Library of Congress Cataloging-in-Publication Data
Names: Case, Jennifer, 1986– author.
Title: Sawbill: a search for place / Jennifer Case.
Description: Albuquerque: University of New Mexico Press, [2018] |
Identifiers: LCCN 2017037417 (print) | LCCN 2017045143 (e-book) |
ISBN 9780826359490 (e-book) | ISBN 9780826359483 (softcover: acid-free paper)
Subjects: LCSH: Case, Jennifer, 1986–
Classification: LCC PS3603.A8393 (e-book) | LCC PS3603.A8393 Z46 2018 (print) |
DDC 813/.6 [B]—dc23
LC record available at https://lccn.loc.gov/2017037417

Cover illustration adapted from photograph by Robert Engberg,
licensed under CC by 2.0
Designed by Felicia Cedillos
Composed in ScalaOT 10.25/14

For my family

Contents

Acknowledgments   ix

SAWBILL   1

BUILDING SAWBILL   17

THE BOUNDARY WATERS   31

BIKING BEHIND DAD   51

SAWBILL MAP   63

ANOTHER SWISS FAMILY ROBINSON   67

HOMEMAKING   73

THE DECKLED EDGE   83

PIECING   91

MOVEMENT   109

E-MAIL FROM GRANDMA   119

ST. CROIX   125

ALONENESS   139

E-MAIL FROM LORI   143

GARDENING WITH RUTH   149

RESEARCH   161

APPALACHIAN TRAIL   167

RETURN TO MINNESOTA 173

SOLBAKKEN 185

REVISITING SAWBILL 199

COOK COUNTY HISTORICAL SOCIETY 211

INTERVIEW WITH DAD 217

INTERVIEW WITH MARY ALICE 225

UNIDENTIFIABLE BIRD 235

INTERIMS 243

Acknowledgments

Many thanks to the editors of the following journals, in which earlier versions of some of these chapters appeared:

Zone 3: "The Deckled Edge."
ISLE: "The Boundary Waters."
Green Hills Literary Lantern: "Piecing."

Thank you to Carrie McHugh and the Cook County Historical Society for their generous assistance and for access to their archives. Thank you to Michael and Maureen, owners of Solbakken, for graciously answering my questions about life on the North Shore, and to Scott for sharing his scrapbook and memories with me. Thank you to Mary Alice Hansen for welcoming me into her Grand Marais home and to my family members, Helen Case, Steven Case, Julie Case, Jeffrey Case, Emily Case, Lori Case, and Lindy Madson for indulging my curiosity and for allowing me to interview them—often multiple times. Many, many thanks to Kevin Lentz for supporting this project, and my career, all along.

I am also grateful for the community of writers of which I've been a part. In particular, I would like to thank Leslie Heywood for first telling me I was writing a book, Hilda Raz for encouraging me to be ambitious, and Alexi Zentner, Maria Gillan, Jeffner Allen, Tom Lynch, Jaimee Wriston Colbert, Trisha Cowen, Barrett Bowlin, Virginia Shank, and Sara Erdmann for their feedback and for the intellectual community they offered when I was drafting this material.

Special thanks to Marissa Schwalm for her thorough and perceptive reading of so many chapters and drafts; to Sarah Chavez for her unfailingly astute comments and her ongoing belief in this project; to Sandy Longhorn, my fellow Midwestern transplant, for her friendship and shared understanding of the importance of place; and to James Engelhardt for his editorial suggestions, his careful listening, and his encouragement. Thank you, as well, to Monica Rentfrow, who never saw the finished manuscript but offered joyous support from the start.

Last, thank you to Elise McHugh and everyone at the University of New Mexico Press for the care and attention they have shown this book.

SAWBILL

IN THE AUTUMN of 2009, when I am twenty-three, I find myself in my father's now dark and dusty office, searching for books about the Boundary Waters Canoe Area and Sawbill Lodge, the rustic fishing resort my grandparents once ran in northern Minnesota. I am alone. Or nearly alone. A few rooms away my mother sleeps off painkillers from a surgery that removed a cancerous skin tumor from her nose. But my father is 2,500 miles away in St. Croix, and my siblings, too, are in other cities, other states.

As I kneel on the floor, I listen for footsteps. As I open boxes of books, I stiffen as if being watched. The boxes are worn, yet the edges sharp, and the books and mementos I search for are surprisingly easy to spot: a photograph of my father with a fish, a how-to guide for backpacking with children, a guide to the Boundary Waters Canoe Area, and a local history book about Sawbill Outfitters. These are books my father bought at Barnes and Noble or ordered online. Books he'd studied, marked up, and packed in the large blue backpack for the camping trips our family of five took. I, in turn, had flipped through them off and on throughout my adolescence and early adulthood—when doing research for a paper or when planning a canoeing trip with my fiancé. Now, they appear in the box just as I'd remembered: the green backpacking guide with the rough, plastic cover; the Boundary Waters guide, the spine now cracked; the history of Sawbill, covered slightly in dust.

I pull out the books and flip through the pages. I fan through the books with my thumb. I think of my father, more than two thousand miles away, and for a moment the fact that he has left the books here gnaws at me. He moved because state deficits caused his university to cut his department, but why wouldn't he bring the books with him, the way I've collected and saved my own memories of those family camping trips? Why wouldn't he at least take them along?

That fall a poetry professor in my graduate program at Nebraska asks me what it is I love most in the world. "Your family?" he suggests, as we sit in his office. "Your fiancé in Michigan?" I redden; stare at my cuticles, the scuffed tips of my shoes. I'm not thinking of anyone. Instead, I am thinking of water—of the Mississippi River valley bluffs in southeast Minnesota and, even more, of the North Shore where my family so often camped when I was younger. The land where I woke early to read books in front of the previous night's campfire, the ash damp with dew, and waited for my father, my mother, and later my fiancé, to emerge from the tent. The land where, for four years, my grandparents ran a small resort. Where my father skinned fish for tourists. Where my uncle once shot a bear.

Now, I can't stop thinking of the resort. As I sit in my dad's office while my mom sleeps, the images grow. I imagine life at Sawbill and create scenes so lively I swear I've lived there myself— that I was the one skinning fish in the shack near the lake; the one pushing off in an aluminum canoe, guiding tourists to the portage; the one driving the twenty-five miles to Tofte to pick up flour and milk.

Like a gas bubble beneath my chest, Sawbill turns physical. It presses against my ribs and expands in my lungs. It colors my memories so that when I think of the North Shore and my family's experiences there, I am thinking of longing, though not always my own. In a world where families routinely move, where fewer and fewer adults stay at one job for longer than a handful of years, my longing for place and permanence forms itself into a stone, moves from my stomach to my lungs to the back of my throat, until all I can do is remember and try to understand.

When I am twenty-three, I live in a one-bedroom apartment in Nebraska while I earn my master's degree. I walk the mile and a half to campus in order to avoid using fossil fuels, and I shop almost exclusively at the local co-op in order to support local farms. The vast sky of the Great Plains fascinates me. I want to learn about this new place. And yet, on weekends, I get in my car and drive fifteen minutes to Pioneer Park, a heavily landscaped tract of land often criticized for its non-native trees. I spend my afternoons meandering the paths and reading by the small man-made lake because the green and the blue, unlike Nebraska's palate of yellows and browns, reminds me of family and of home.

My family camped often when I was young, and once my siblings and I were old enough, we began backpacking along the North Shore. Twice a summer for four or five summers, we packed our backpacks and drove up to the North Shore—a three- to six-hour trek depending on where we hiked. Each and every time my father became a different man. "I can feel the stress leaving," he said to my mother, beside him in the passenger seat. My father wore a T-shirt and slippery pants with zip-off legs instead of a dress shirt and tie. He wasn't answering the phone or rushing off to a meeting or packing for a business trip that would take him to a computer engineering convention in Baltimore or a consultation in China. He wasn't leaving early in the morning and coming back after we'd gone to bed. Instead, he played road games with us. We yelled out the letters of the alphabet as we spotted them on road signs. We held our breath when driving through tunnels. "If you make it, your wish will come true," my dad told us, though toward the end of each tunnel he grinned at our bulging cheeks and pressed the brake.

On the North Shore we skipped stones in Lake Superior and played card games. We hiked in a single-file line through thin trails carpeted with pine needles. The land was the most beautiful I'd seen: red rocks, overlooks where Lake Superior, the largest of the Great Lakes, appeared like a glimmer on the horizon, past the rolling landscape of deep, green trees. I swung my arms and didn't complain about blisters and was so deeply happy I felt my face would explode.

We backpacked for three or four days and then stayed at state parks, where we waded near waterfalls and toured historic lighthouses. Sometimes we took day trips to Grand Marais or Grand Portage, and once, after a weekend of rain, we visited the area where my father grew up. My parents herded us with our muddy boots and dripping ponchos into the family van and drove twenty or so miles away from Lake Superior, toward the easternmost lakes of the Boundary Waters. We stopped in a parking lot devoid of people, a parking lot filled only with a few rows of cars, some Boy Scout trailers, and a line of three porta potties near the rear.

While my siblings chased each other, I followed my father fifteen feet from the van and looked into the dense forest. He pointed out where a lodge had once stood—a clearing closed up with trees. Most of the cabins were gone as well—only a few small fishing huts remained, each no bigger than a one-car garage. I had to squint to see the brown buildings, so decomposed that they blended with the trees.

"It sure has changed," he said, his hands stuffed in his pockets.

It's an image I cling to, now that I live in Nebraska and my father has moved from Minnesota to St. Croix: my father with his tanned arms and muscular thighs, his T-shirt and khakis, the darkness of the brush and the shadows that I want to believe held us there, just the two of us, until we became a part of the mist, the trees.

The day after my mom's surgery, we order Chinese for dinner. I pour shrimp fried rice into two salad bowls. To ease the silence, I focus on eating as slowly as possible. I sip wine between each bite; move the fork against the bottom of the bowl without scraping the porcelain. The family dog, a shepherd-husky mix recently diagnosed with liver disease, farts in a corner of the living room. Scared by the smell, he pushes himself up and hobbles on bony shoulders to another corner, where he collapses with a thud. Though my mother's surgery is successful, a minor procedure without a lasting impact on her health, the situation unnerves me. She is alone, teaching at the local elementary school in case my dad doesn't like St. Croix. She tells me she sometimes takes sleeping pills at night. She wishes my father could come back home.

"It's nice to have someone else in this creaky house," she says.

I bite the lip of my wineglass. When the dog farts again and heaves himself onto shaking feet, I call him to my side. I run my hand down his knobby spine and try not to think of my mother alone all winter in the drafty house, with the gassy dog, contacting family only through e-mails and phone lines and wireless towers.

Instead, I return to my father's office and pick up the local history book titled *Sawbill: History and Tales*. The book jacket, designed to look like birch bark, displays images of families and canoes, a black and white lodge, and a moose. It is a book I read briefly a while back but not one I've returned to since.

There, on his office floor, I flip to the chapter on Sawbill Lodge and skim for our last name. I find it on page seventy-eight. "Charles and Helen Case," the book says, purchased the lodge in the early 1970s, when my father was still in secondary school.

They looked forward to retiring in a few years and living full-time at Sawbill. However, Chuck, who was a sales engineer with AT&T, was drawn into his career more than he ever anticipated. His last sale before his scheduled retirement was an internal telephone system for Honeywell in London, England. He became involved in installing the new system and then was hired by Honeywell to run the system. His plans to retire did not come about and running the Lodge was far too demanding while he was commuting to London.

According to the book, my grandparents gave up the lodge after only a few years.

The next paragraphs talk about the following owners—the Sentys from Madison, Wisconsin. They too, it seems, stayed at the lodge for only a short time, though Mary Alice Hansen, the author of the book and founder of Sawbill Outfitters, gives the Sentys an entire page, instead of just a paragraph, before moving to the lodge's auction in 1983, when it was dismantled and the original resort returned to forest.

The brevity of the passage unnerves me. Surely my family had just as much of a claim to the history as anyone else. Surely there must be more. I keep a finger in the page that talks about my grandparents and flip forward and back, but our last name—as if we have no stake in the place, as if we are not important—does not appear again.

I stare at the pictures, the back cover where Mary Alice and her husband smile in matching pink shirts, both wearing glasses,

Mary Alice as white-haired as my grandmother. I turn to page seventy-nine, where "Helen Case" pops on the first line, followed by the "four children" that includes my two aunts, my uncle, and my dad. I once asked my dad why the passage was so short. His only response: "Your grandma and Mary Alice didn't get along."

At first his statement piqued me. Maybe there was some deep grudge, some secret that could tie us even more firmly to this place.

But now the paragraph unsettles me. It doesn't explain the way my father looked at the woods that time in the parking lot, the way my body lightens at overlooks. It doesn't imply that we belong there—somewhere—and will always come back.

When my mother calls me, I leave the room and slip the book into my bag.

A memory: I am twenty-one and my family is driving to the North Shore for "one last" family vacation. When we were younger this trip had seemed routine. We'd load the back of the van with our backpacks, stop in Duluth to stretch our legs, and hold our breath for good luck as we drove through the tunnels on Highway 61. Now that it's been four years since we've gone together, I wonder if this is the last time we'll all come up. I clench my stomach against a sudden hollowness. As the interstate climbs one last, familiar hill, however, I sit straighter. Lake Superior flashes on the horizon—a strip of glistening light deep in the valley. Brake lights flicker as the interstate then dips, following the steep descent into the harbor. Narrow homes cling to hills, and in the distance a barge passes beneath the lift bridge.

My mom and sister both put down their books and look out the windows. Even my brother, over six feet tall and asleep in the front seat, wakes up from his nap. "How far until the tunnel?" my sister asks.

"A while," my dad replies. He rests an arm against the window and starts to hum.

The highway curves to the left past Canal Park where we'd always stop to skip stones when younger. We swing past downtown Duluth, with its brick storefronts, its train museum, and the circular hotel with the rotating restaurant on the top floor.

My dad reaches back and rests a hand on my mom's knee.

We're surrounded by houses—stately buildings next to the shore that have been turned into nursing homes and law offices. Lake Superior glints between the trees and crashes against the red rocks.

"Now how far?" my sister asks.

We curve past a string of motels and a new resort. A billboard advertises Canoe Country Outfitters and then another for the outfitters nearest Sawbill Lake.

"Two more miles!" my dad calls out. "Get ready!"

We straighten in our seats and adjust our seatbelts.

"One and a half miles!"

My sister pokes my brother on the shoulder.

"One mile!"

And there it is—the Silver Bay tunnel, one of three tunnels the highway department carved through what's left of the Sawtooth Mountains. The dark opening looms and my dad grins. "Get ready!"

In one motion, my father, mother, brother, sister, and I inhale until our lungs press against our ribs. We lock our lips and teeth the moment the car enters the tunnel. Lights whiz past us. Engines and tires echo through the chamber. Our faces redden as the line of cars and their taillights curve to the right. We search for the opening at the end of the tunnel. Our cheeks puff. We grimace as our hearts thump against our chests. Still no opening. Ribs and lungs and diaphragms clamp into a single ache at the back of our throats.

My sister scrunches her face in pain and wiggles her head. She points her finger, jabs frantically at a small prick of light in the distance. We stare at my dad, frown as our throats burn, as our eyes press against their sockets. An RV speeds past us on the left. The truck pulling a boat gains ground on us in front. The opening grows. Now we can make out water and rock, the guardrails at the edge of the road. My dad lifts his foot, presses it against the brake. The car slows, the opening barely getting wider. The thinning crown of my dad's head bobbles with a silent glee.

My sister pounds her feet against the bottom of the car. I press my fingers into my knees. My mom slaps my dad's forearm with the back of her hand and my sister uses the last of her air to squeal. My dad accelerates, thrusting us into the sunlight and pine-filled air, where five synchronized expulsions roar from five open mouths. My dad laughs so hard he wipes a tear from his eye.

Another memory: I am in my parent's garage, sorting through camping supplies. I have just graduated from college and have asked my boyfriend to go to the Boundary Waters with me. "My grandparents ran a resort up there for a while," I tell Kevin. "It's wonderful! You'll love it." We plan a weeklong trip and purchase a permit to enter at Brule Lake, just a dozen miles northeast of Sawbill.

In preparation I set aside the bear canisters, two Therm-a-Rest pads, and two down sleeping bags. I pull out two camping mugs as well as six Nalgene bottles. In another bin I find a map. The map highlights Sawbill Lake, with Brule in the top right. Half of Brule, however, is cut off by the margin. I put the map back.

When my dad returns from work that evening, I ask if he had a map of Brule. His shoulders are hunched, his face slack. He doesn't think his department in Minnesota will survive budget cuts much longer. He has started talking about other job openings, including one in St. Croix. For an hour we kneel on the floor, searching through boxes, but we cannot find another map.

"Do you wish you were coming?" I ask. "You could, you know."

My father almost smiles, so that one side of his half-white goatee sticks out. "Kind of. But you'll have fun." Perhaps it is natural: my father letting go. Perhaps the sadness I feel in the moment is nostalgia. I am clinging to my childhood, not ready to move on. But if it is nostalgia, it is a deep nostalgia. A nostalgia laced with something like bliss.

When Kevin and I start out the next week, I am giddy. As we pack the car and stop for gas and drive and drive and drive, the only thing I want is to arrive—to *be* there. I want him to see the shipyards, the lift bridge, the way the land dips dramatically into the harbor, the way the thin houses brace themselves against the slopes. I want him to see Canal Park, where children sift through stones for agates. I want him to hold his breath through the tunnels as we make our way through Duluth and turn northeast onto Highway 61. I want to wrap him in the familiar, make him love the landscape I long to claim, as if it could ground us, our feet together on the red rock, our tongues tasting the scent of pine.

When we near Duluth, I can hardly contain myself. I stuff my hands beneath my thighs and bounce in my seat once we finally dip into the harbor. "Look!" I say. "Look!" Because there it is: layers of memory and family camping trips and stops at the train museum, where we sucked on stick candy, and walks along the shore and skipping stones and an air so full and cool I close my eyes and gulp.

At some point, I ask my dad to tell me about the resort. I do not remember when I asked, or where. I cannot place myself at a particular kitchen table—the round Formica of my parent's kitchen in south central Minnesota or the small, wooden table at my apartment in Nebraska. When I think back to the moment, I can't even remember the color of the walls. I only know that it was probably morning—the one time my dad and I, the two early risers, had to ourselves. So often I've woken to find him in the kitchen already, his laptop on the table, his soup bowl-sized mug of coffee steaming. I join him, and the two of us silently read the newspaper and complete word puzzles as we wait for others to awake. "Need more?" he asks, lifting his mug, and I shake my head, comfortable that that's all we need to say.

So of course I would have asked him about the resort in the morning. I would have rolled the question on my tongue as I had all week, all year. I would have cupped my mug of coffee, worked half-heartedly through a Sudoku puzzle, and waited for him to lift his head.

This much makes sense to me, so it is his response that catches me, engrains itself word for word in my mind. The way he looked over the top of his laptop and then the top of his glasses, his eyes yellow near the edges, the veins red and thick. "No. It was a long time ago. I don't remember much." And even more, I recall my reaction. How quickly I had changed the subject, had let my question slip to the floor. How quickly I had returned to my puzzle or set down the mug that had begun to burn into my palms.

Now, I wish I could press my hand against my younger back, that soft dip between shoulder blades, and encourage myself to continue. Because I need to know how he felt when he first arrived every summer. Whether it was contentment or joy. And I want it to be joy. I want him to have closed his eyes and set his hands on the ground, felt the air expand in his lungs. In the shed, when he skinned fish for tourists, I want the scales to have glistened on his thumb.

More than anything, when I ask him about Sawbill, I need him to miss it—with a sadness that hits him in the gut. So that I know—as I've always needed and wanted to know—that we'll never extricate ourselves from the place or each other.

One year after my father moves to St. Croix, Kevin and I pack our own moving truck and drive from the Midwest to upstate New York. We are moving for job opportunities. For professional advancement. In doing so, we are further detaching from place. For three days we caravan from Nebraska to Indiana and then Ohio to Pennsylvania, flipping through radio stations, pulling off at rest stops for chocolate and coffee, driving and stopping and driving until my back aches before I even get in the car.

Once we arrive, the distance between us and my family, spread out now across so many states, feels so vast, I see everything through a film of displacement. Even a trip to the grocery store, with its florescent lights and unchartered aisles, leaves me shaky. To counter my discomfort, I ask my grandma for photographs of Sawbill. Four days later, a large manila envelope from Missouri arrives in the mail. I am surprised by the speed, though I shouldn't be. My grandparents are moving again, this time to a new senior center. And like all their other moves in recent years—to Utah for the weather, to Missouri for cheaper housing—she must downsize. I have received three boxes in the past week, each stuffed with items my grandma thought I might want: a quilt, a stack of vegetarian cookbooks, a great-great grandmother's green handkerchief. This time I rip open the envelope to find a short note with her new address and a plastic bag filled with the photographs I'd requested.

I carry the bag to the second bedroom, which Kevin and I have turned into an office, and pull out a stack of postcards from the 1960s. Worn on the edges, they depict black-and-white scenes of the log cabins and stone fireplaces. My grandma also includes photographs she took in the 1970s—square images, grainier and with purple tinges on the edges. She has written descriptions on the back:

A day's catch on Sawbill.
Dock Boy—Bob(?) Johnston
One of the Fireplaces in the Lodge. It is huge.

The ink was still wet when she stacked the photos to send them, and some of the images stick together.

I flip through the photographs and then study each one. Bob Johnston, a gangly teenager in a red football T-shirt, heaps potatoes onto a plate. In the "day's catch" photograph, what could be an older Bob Johnston, or another man altogether, stands next to a wide-hipped man. The possible Bob holds a string of seven walleye. The older man holds a string of four smallmouth bass.

Beneath these, my grandma has clipped five photographs together and labeled them with a Post-it: *The Drive up to Sawbill from Tofte. 25 Miles.* In three of these images, gravel roads lead through pine. In the other two, snow covers a road void of tire tracks.

I draw my knees toward my chest and lean back in the chair. The water and trees are familiar to me even if the individual scenes are not. In a postcard labeled "Sawbill Lake from Dining Room," pine trees frame a view of a placid lake, a sky light with cumulus clouds. It looks much like the photographs Kevin and I took while camping on Brule Lake—using roots and tree trunks to pull ourselves onto rock overlooks. That slightly waving land, green and lush with water. Looking at the images, I can almost feel pine needles beneath my feet, the sun on my back, the chill of a breeze. For a moment, as I close my eyes and smile, I can almost hear that zippered skim of paddle on water.

I set the photographs in a pile on the floor, along with the history book by Mary Alice Hansen that I recently purchased, photographs from my own trips up north, my journals with dog-eared pages. All summer, the pile of notes and envelopes and paper has grown, the place becoming a reality, at least in the sense that there is proof it was once there.

But I am not in any pictures of Sawbill itself. In the single photograph I have of his family at the resort, my dad, curly haired and thin, braces his arms against the railing of a brown porch and squints into the woods. His mouth is open, revealing the gap between his two front teeth. He is familiar with the cool summer air, the scent of pine. Less than six years later, he will propose to my mother in a state park not far from that porch. Less than thirty years after that, following our four-day trip on Brule Lake, Kevin and I will discuss marriage near the same park. Yet I have no memory of the lodge, the cabins, the lake. I can pretend to be part of the story—to have a family history cut into the granite of those shores—but in the end, aside from that short stop in the boat launch parking lot when I was ten, I have nothing physical to claim.

Instead, I sit in this chair, near this window, more than a thousand miles from the boat launch and the now-dilapidated cabins, and feel empty even of stories, the very things that root us, that tell us who and where we are. I have no stories here, and even more unnerving, I have no stories of Sawbill. How can I write of Sawbill when I was only there for twenty minutes? When I have no idea if I, or my family, will ever go back? Apparently, my grandma and father filleted fish from the lake, shoveled the lake effect snow, and watched black bear scour the county landfill. All I can do is reach back through the decades, but even then, I can't help but think I'm grasping at nothing, dreaming of a rootedness that will never exist.

My parents, tired of living apart, have said they will move next year. My father will apply to university jobs in the continental US, and wherever he ends up, my mother will join him. My sister, like so many young professionals, is graduating from college and considering job opportunities in nine different states. Some evenings, when Kevin and I read on the couch, I lean into him and ask where we'll be in five years. We imagine homes in Duluth, St. Paul, Marquette—places where water laps against rock. But when I'm alone in our apartment, the images are hesitant, hollow. I'll have to find work as an English professor where he can find work at a museum. I know not to expect much. When it comes to a homeplace, this version of Sawbill is as close as I can get.

I pick up the local history book and smooth the cream pages. I reread the paragraph my family receives. My grandparents, Hansen writes, had planned to retire at the lodge. They planned to run the resort in the summers and enjoy the last of their days fishing from the dock. The words pull at me—the hook of a fishing line snagged in my ribs. And so I follow them. I grip the thin line, wrap it twice around my wrist, and let it drag me into the depths of questions I need answered: the relationship between place and family, how movement disrupts that, and what we must do as a result to best live on this earth.

BUILDING SAWBILL

🎋 EARLY INTO MY infatuation with Sawbill, while I am still living in Nebraska, I come across a simple metaphor that Lawrence Buell, an environmental critic, uses to think about place. I find the description in the first chapter of a book on environmental literature, and, as I sit in my apartment, my mother in Minnesota and my dad in St. Croix, it seems to suddenly explain my longing.

Cultures of earlier times, Buell says, had a sense of place akin to concentric rings. At its center was a home that they knew well— the intimately known region where they lived and worked—and the further they distanced themselves from that point, the less they felt bonded to the environment.

In contrast, today—in an era of modernization and globalization—Buell argues that we hop from location to location, which causes that sense of place as concentric rings to instead take the shape of an archipelago. We know a small place, and work at another small place, and move to another small place, but those locations are islands, isolated from one another. Our understanding of the world is stretched out and thinned.

My family, I realize, is living on islands. We have lost an

intimately known homeland and the sense of bonding it would have provided.

When I first sit down to read about the Argobust family and to find where the story of Sawbill began, I, as a result, expect to encounter concentric rings: information about people who built the lodge and loved it. People who poured their sweat into the making of the area—the roads and the lodges that then, in the early 1900s, were considered one of the "unsettled" parts of the United States. People who devoted so much work to the area that they stayed. Because that is the assumption made by so many of the environmental writers I love: Aldo Leopold, Wendell Berry, and Scott Russell Sanders. Physical labor and local knowledge creates a profound and beautiful bond, allowing you to enter into a community, and if you devote yourself enough to a location, it becomes impossible for you to separate yourself from it. "People who stay in place may come to know that place more deeply. People who know a place may come to care about it more deeply. People who care *about* a place are more likely to take better care of it," Robert Thayer Jr. writes, and I believe him. Or at least I want to. I recognize how much environmental harm results from lifestyles that don't facilitate that kind of attention and care. Environmental harm that results from the way my own family pops through airports, hardly noticing where we are, how the noise patterns of the planes might affect certain neighborhoods, how the coffee we drink from disposable cups is affecting farmers in Latin America and landfills here. How the histories of the regions we live in and travel through—great swaths of the Midwest, southeast, and even Caribbean—might require more thoughtful uses of our natural resources.

Surely, the Argobusts, builders of Sawbill lodge, which my family once ran, were people who cared. And by researching them, I expect to find a family that might serve as a parallel to my own, had my own been transported to something other than the twenty-first century, when the world erupted into movement: those transcontinental flights, international job postings, the average American working nearly a dozen jobs over the course of a lifetime. In the Argobusts, I expect groundedness. A perhaps more settled understanding of how the world works and how family functions.

And at first, the Argobusts do seem to offer that parallel. Theirs is a story about longing. About the way a place can drag you in, can bring your arms to the ground, your knees to the rocky soil. About place as a way to locate and center family.

Before Sawbill, the Argobusts were scattered. Strewn across the Midwest, they struggled to survive. George lost his job in Ohio, his wife died, and suddenly he had five kids he couldn't feed as the world slumped into the 1930s and the Great Depression. George moved his family to Chicago in search of employment, but even there—in that vastly unfamiliar cityscape—they struggled. Eventually they moved to Wisconsin, where George left the kids in a cabin during the days. The children played by the lake and fended for themselves. They were happy. But when the authorities discovered five kids not enrolled in school, the Argobusts returned to Chicago.

Yet their second try at a large city was no better than the first. George couldn't find work. The oldest children sold newspapers and magazines door-to-door in order to eke out some sort of existence in the world they had. They were drifters in need of place. In need of grounding.

Reading their history, I am simultaneously saddened and pulled in.

After I move to Nebraska and my father moves to St. Croix, our family struggles to get together. That first summer I can't get back to Minnesota until August. By that point, my father will have returned to St. Croix and my sister will already be back at college. My mom calls me in July, when my siblings and dad are home. We play a game of Yahtzee on speakerphone; my siblings, Jeff and Emily, bicker in the background.

"Well, we should probably let you go," my mom says after the game. "We wish you were here." I slump in my chair and stare at the parking lot outside my window. As I think of my family's movement, my own movement, and what I am and am not prioritizing in my life, I wonder what it means to live a life of disconnection—what it means to not commit to a place. When I read about George Argobust and his decision to move from Ohio, I can't help but wonder if he saw in his own family the kind of wandering and discontentment that Scott Russell Sanders describes when quietly, purposefully, trying to tell us about the deprivations experienced by "those who have no parish, those who navigate ceaselessly among postal zones and area codes, those for whom the world is only a smear of highways and bank accounts and stores."

I'd like to think so, which is why it makes sense to me that in 1931, Wilson and George Jr., the older brothers, left Chicago and headed north in search of new, more permanent opportunities. "We intended to earn money for the family," Wilson wrote in straightforward prose, in his six-page autobiography about the founding of Sawbill Lodge. They decided to head to the northeastern corner of Minnesota, where Wilson had fished with his uncle at Gateway Lodge on the Gunflint Trail. They hoped to find work there and eventually start a resort of their own. So they loaded up a knapsack with apples and bread, spent nights in freight cars, and caught rides from strangers. They traveled through land my family knows well—Red Wing, Minnesota, and then St. Paul—as if pulled by the memory of the North Shore: the jagged red rock, the white birch and poplar. It's almost, I think, as if the area had imprinted itself onto Wilson's memory. The North Shore, for Wilson, like me, becomes an ideal place.

Writers of place argue that emplacement heals the wounds of

displacement. That settling down offers spiritual rewards. "In belonging to a landscape," Scott Russell Sanders writes, "one feels a rightness, at homeness, a knitting of self and world." He compares this sense of belonging and at homeness to "what the Buddhists call mindfulness, what Christian contemplatives refer to as recollection, what Quakers call centering down." In other words, place can ground us in more ways than one. It can give us concentric rings instead of islands.

I wish for Wilson that centeredness. The same centeredness I wish for myself. In the few photographs I have of Wilson, he is a lanky teenager, thin and slightly awkward in the way of most young adults. He wears white T-shirts and baggy, khaki pants. Though most of his hair is close-cropped, his thick bangs form a cowlick. He braces his elbows against his sides while holding a large bass, or smiles into the camera, an arm around his brothers. He deserves that happiness, so I give it to him. In my imagination, as I sit in my apartment in Nebraska and later upstate New York, his story—spliced across newspaper articles and oral histories—glows as if lit by dreams:

In 1931, just south of Duluth, heat shimmered above the road. The land rose slowly, the oaks and maples giving away to birch and pine. Wilson elbowed his brother as the truck that had picked them up made its way up one final mound. At the top, Lake Superior suddenly burst into view, the thin angle of its harbor visible like a blue lash deep in the valley. Barges filled the docks, steel machinery emptying ore into their tanks. Trains chugged along the shore, toward the port, and thin rows of houses braced themselves against the hills.

The boys leaned forward as the trucker sailed down the hill into the city with its dockyard and brick buildings and train stations. The air cooled, and Wilson could almost taste the coldness of the lake on his tongue. "Hey, Chub. If you wade in that lake, your feet will turn blue," Wilson said to George Jr., who grinned back at him, just as my siblings and I had grinned at my father in the family van.

The idea of a wilderness area forming a sort of ideal is not new. Environmental writers, from Thoreau to John Muir to Edward Abbey to Annie Dillard have all, to a degree, purposefully left cities to try and prove themselves in nature, to enter an environment in search of insight and wisdom. Minnesota's North Shore—in the 1930s and today—isn't altogether different from those other iconic landscapes: Thoreau's Walden Pond, Muir's mountains, Abbey's Arches National Park. Until the 1930s, highways did not extend to Minnesota's northeastern lakes. Indeed, it was the Civilian Conservation Corps, an organization that believed physical, wilderness experiences could turn urban boys into men, that built much of the area's first infrastructure.

In the American cultural imagination, the North Shore is a place of respite and retreat as well as a proving ground. The Boundary Waters Canoe Area and the Gunflint Trail host wilderness trips that entail hunting, fishing, canoeing, and backpacking. All require some sort of physical strength and the perhaps faulty belief that we are survivors, capable of sustaining ourselves in harsh environments. And harsh it is. Northeastern Minnesota is often the coldest in the continental United States. The *Edmund Fitzgerald* sank off of Lake Superior's shores. Lake Superior is the deepest, most frigid of the Great Lakes.

My own attraction to the North Shore, both as a child and now an adult, stems from that cultural allure. Tourists still visit the area with sleeping bags and canoes, with high-performance jackets, with carefully designed hiking boots. Even today, in the twenty-first century, the resorts don't take groups kayaking on windy days. Yet even today, canoeists get stranded and need rescuing. The danger, in fact, becomes part of the appeal. At the North Shore, we can get away from cars and cell phones, back into nature—to the aspen and birch, the sunsets reflected on water, where human life is both magnified and minimized. Where living in place *does* require specific, technical survival skills. Where the need for that knowledge presses on the back of your neck as you sleep.

If I want to feel part of a place, in the way that Sanders felt part of a place, to burrow myself in its history, to commit myself to its beauty and risks, this is where I would do it. This, I sense, is where the Argobusts would do it, too.

Wilson and his brother George Jr. arrived in northeastern Minnesota only to discover from a truck driver that Gateway Lodge had burned down in a fire. Dejected, they spent the night in a fishing house in Tofte before catching a ride to nearby Hungry Jack Lake, where they hiked three miles to Gateway Lodge in the hopes they could at least help the owners rebuild.

Those last three miles brought back memories for Wilson. He recalled the summer fishing trip with his uncle. Those warm and carefree days before his mother's death. The ease of those memories grated against the long days of hitchhiking with his brother and the desire to escape the cramped apartment in Chicago. When Wilson and George Jr. finally arrived, Sue and Jesse Gapen greeted them warmly, offering food. But they could only take on one of the boys as an employee. In a conversation I can only imagine, Wilson and his brother decided that Wilson would stay at Gateway while his brother would return home.

Though Wilson mentions little of his time with the Gapens in his six-page autobiography, it is clear he still wanted the northwoods to reunite his family. As he and the other hired men felled trees on West Bearskin Lake, pushed and pulled and maneuvered the felled logs into the water, floated them across the lake, and portaged them a mile to the burnt remains of Gateway Lodge, Wilson continued to dream of a resort of his own. On Saturday evenings, when the other men drove into Grand Marais, he stayed at Gateway and practiced peeling the logs with a draw knife. He watched his muscles strengthen, and every month, he sent most of his $15 pay back to his father in Chicago, waiting for the bits of news he received in reply: *Chub and Hedge found work at a grocery store. They get paid in food. I've met a woman. Marriage is a possibility.*

That January, Wilson hitchhiked back to Chicago to confront his father and his father's soon-to-be second wife. Although the rest of the Argobust children had taken to Jean immediately, Wilson eyed her with distrust. Nonetheless, Jean held her ground. The only female graduate of Cornell University's program in hotel management, she was accustomed to intimidation—to closed doors she must heave open. Sawbill, in fact, became Jean and Wilson's neutral zone—the one thing they had in common. Jean's background in hotel management proved an asset that Wilson could support.

All January they spoke about it—at the small table in his father's apartment, the five kids huddled around, faces glowing in the low light like they used to, George at the one end of the table, hands pressed to his nose, and Jean at the other. She showed them the books she still had from college, the plans she'd laid out—the steps they'd have to take to get started.

They spoke about schooling for the youngest Argobust children: Harry, Jane, and Robert. About telephones and electricity and running water. About financing and attracting guests. Sometimes, the setbacks must have felt so large, both Jean and Wilson thought they'd give up.

But in the end, the seven of them—Jean and George, Wilson and George Jr., Harry, Jane, and Robert—decided to give it a try.

A week later, Wilson returned to Gateway, only this time with more purpose. As the Gapens rebuilt the lodge, Wilson etched what he saw into his head for future reference. He used a compass to mark the lines in the logs. The lines guided the ax when they grooved lengthwise, cutting notches for corner fits. He watched the Swedish workers use the double-blade ax to make the notches and grooves. They used the broad ax for steps and the fireplace mantel. They leaned into each other, rocking their feet, building momentum.

After supper, when the other men retreated to the bunkhouse and the wind moved like a whisper through the trees, Wilson carried the axes to the refuse pile. The abandoned ends of the Norway pines froze to the ground, a mountain in the snow. Wilson kicked at them, unearthed them, wiped ice off of wood with his hand. The logs gleamed in the night. He pushed and pulled, strained and sweated, felt the edge of the ax nip into the wood.

With those hands and those tools, he would make of this place a livelihood, a home.

George is the only family member involved with the building of Sawbill that I cannot readily understand—or at least cannot readily place in my imaginative rendering of that time period. He exists on the sidelines, someone whose involvement is less enthusiastic. He doesn't seem to have been drawn to Sawbill with the same force—to have seen it as a place that offered centering. Instead, it was mostly an opportunity, and perhaps an opportunity that required an energy he didn't have.

When George and Jean married in April, they decided to head north near Wilson. From the various oral histories that exist, it is clear that Jean made many of the plans. She wrote letters to friends she had in New York and asked for advice, while George, it appears, followed along, attracted largely to the stability that Jean provided his family. In fact, it was Jean's old car that they drove to Tofte, where they learned a new road had just been built to a lake called

Sawbill. The forest service suggested Jean and George look for a resort site there.

That weekend Wilson came down from Gateway and the three of them drove Jean's Nash the twenty-four miles to Sawbill. Halfway in, the spring melt turned the gravel to mud. The Nash got mired. The wheels spit mud and stone backward but did not move. George and Wilson got out and pushed. Mud seeped up their pant legs. George slipped and the mud seeped to his knee. Rain began to fall. They managed to extract the car, only to "hump and grind on" for two more hours.

Finally, they stopped near a stream—the Temperance River. They waded into the stream and along the shore, Wilson and then Jean and then George, until the stream met the lake.

The view stunned Wilson and Jean. The land rose from the lake and then flattened out, a few areas already patchy with grass. Hundreds of tall trees lined the lake and the lodge site, creating an oasis of water in the woods. "We were thrilled and excited," Wilson wrote later. "This certainty was the right place."

George did not say anything. Or, at least, no oral histories exist. His reaction is lost. And in the absence, I envision apathy. I wonder if George shared the group's joy—if the view hooked itself into his chest wall in the way it must have hooked itself into both Wilson's and Jean's. Or if, instead, he had expected more: the start of a building, or at least a cabin, rather than the stony shore, the uplift in the land, and the darkness of the trees. For a man who had already begun new lives in four different states, what energy could he take to another beginning? How many times can we start over again?

I would not blame him for exhaustion.

In 1933 work began. Wilson quit his job at Gateway and joined George and Jean in Tofte. The step forward elated Wilson, though the pace continued to prove agonizingly slow. In what Wilson calls the "almost unendurable" months during which George and Jean struggled to secure permission from the forest service and a loan from the bank, Wilson shrunk and seethed. The knife he used to skin fish turned clumsy. He cut the wrong parts, chopped the wood the wrong size. To keep his sanity, he guided day trips west to Alton, Beth, and Grace Lake, then north to Ada and Cherokee, or east to Smoke, Burnt, and Kelly. "We found the fishing to be unexcelled, wild, rewarding, exciting beyond compare. The forest, the lakes, rivers unbelievably beautiful, many to be 'discovered' and explored," Wilson wrote. The water calmed him as it must have calmed my father when he was young. Wilson dipped his paddle into the lake, skimmed his hands on the surface. He paddled hard, the front of the canoe slicing though the water without a sound. Last year's leaves floated near the banks, and lily pads made a green sheen of the marshes.

In the winter, Wilson's uncle paid for his schooling in Minneapolis, where Wilson met an architecture student. Wilson showed the student his father's drawings of rock outcroppings, land levels, and trees and convinced him to draw up a design. In the weak light of the winter, with coffee and sandwiches, Wilson and the architect dreamed up the entire complex—the lodge, the log cabins, the guest dormitory, the dock and canoe racks, the living quarters . . . even a freshwater well. The planning and drafting carried him through the winter, until Jean and George finally got permission to start.

That summer, Wilson lost himself in the work. He and the others dug the foundation for the lodge and set it in concrete with cedar timbers. They scouted the lake for Norway or white pine, but they could only locate jack pine—knottier than they wanted, but still sturdy.

Tony, the hired man, and Wilson used the six-foot, two-person saw to cut eighteen trees a day. They carried the saw fifty feet off-shore, sawed until wood cracked and sweat ran down their foreheads. Once each tree fell, they topped it, limbed it, and then dragged it to the shore. From a distance, those white and brown logs looked like a pile of matchsticks haphazardly scattered in the dirt. But close up, the magnitude of those four hundred and thirty-four logs pulled knees to the ground.

George borrowed a fishing boat from Andy Tofte, a member of the township's founding family, and towed six or seven logs at a time the five and a half miles to the lodge site. The progress was slow. When snow and ice began to fall in November, white trunks still lined the bank. Snow flicked the water like mosquitoes, eventually giving the entire shore an icy top layer. Wilson and the crew pulled their collars up and listened for the chug of the three-horsepower motor. George hauled one load of logs, then told the crew to pack up. They filled the boat with the tents and sleeping bags, the saws and axes. Just before dark, when George came back one last time, the crew themselves jumped in. As they chugged away into darkness, the fifty-some logs they left behind bobbed on the water, their tops already white with snow.

The next morning, when Wilson returned to the logs, they had frozen within the ice. At the sight, George let the motor die. Snow blew across the lake, whistling through the air with an eerie whine. If the logs remained another night, they'd be stuck all winter. The group unloaded hatchets and picks. For twelve hours straight, they gouged ice from the frozen pine until each of the logs again bobbed like an icy martyr. Then, in trip after trip, they hauled the logs to the other side of the lake and pulled them to the shore. Once they had finally salvaged all of the logs, the men collapsed on the bank as Jean brought out blankets and hot coffee. They were too exhausted to talk, but already they could see it: Sawbill Lodge, up on the hill like a dream.

It's a beautiful moment in the story. The ice. The snow. The logs.

The logs sitting there, the pieces all set for assembly. The story about to unfold and take place. It's enough to make me want to stop my research, to say, "Here! Here it is! This is the story we must follow." They put in the work. They found a way to make their dreams unfold. Their love for the area, their care for the place, surely, is palpable. And in caring for the place, didn't they do what so many families during the Great Depression and so many families today cannot? Didn't they manage to come back together? To create their own community in a place that they loved? Community with the environment and with each other?

And yet, maybe it was only in that moment of anticipation that Sawbill seemed perfect, for me and for them. For it is in the opening of the lodge, and its history after, that my expectations for centeredness flounder.

The Argobusts opened Sawbill Lodge in 1935, to minimal success. They sent one hundred postcards a day to Minneapolis businessmen whose addresses they got through George's brother's advertising agency. Not all of the businessmen came, but some did. Wilson and his brothers guided them on fishing trips and hunting expeditions. Jean cooked fish, roast venison, potatoes, vegetables, and bread. There was always coffee and apples, cookies and donuts for dessert. The guests liked to sit in front of the fireplaces in the evenings, and sometimes the Argobusts would join them for a game of chess or checkers. It seemed promising.

But contrary to all of my hopes and expectations, the Argobusts' stay didn't last long.

When 1941 came around and the Japanese bombed Pearl Harbor, the stint at Sawbill was over. The Argobusts tried to keep the lodge open that summer, but it was harder to get supplies, and with gas rationing, fewer and fewer guests arrived.

All the boys but Wilson joined the services. One in the Navy, two in the Air Corps. Even the daughter left to join the Woman's Army Corps. Though Wilson couldn't enlist because of bad hearing, he built military seaports and warehouses in the Aleutian Islands. By the time the war ended, the Argobust children had started lives elsewhere and never returned. "We were all scattered and there was no home to go back to," Jane, the youngest Argobust, later wrote.

After 1942, Jean left Sawbill too. She returned to Chicago and took a job as chief dietician for US Airways. George left for Duluth. The divorce came later.

And so the location that was always meant to keep the family together failed—just as it would fail to keep my family in one place decades later, as much as I wanted it to. Sawbill was not the center of a series of concentric rings but rather one stop along a string of locations and homelands. In my romantic visions of the resort's birth, then, I must remind myself of its end—of the comings and goings that have defined it all along. Maybe Wilson did form a strong attachment, an attachment I would like to believe mirrors my father's or my own. But he left Sawbill, and for whatever reason, it could not reel him in again.

In fact, only Jean returned. As if the land had imprinted itself in her, forcing her to dream of birch and pine, the lodge pulled her back. After the war ended, she returned to the dirt road and the two fireplaces and the cabins with their sanded jack pine beams. She reinstated the lease and contacted old clients. Jane, the youngest Argobust, stopped by every once in a while to say hello and help out, but in the end only Jean lived the rest of her life in the area. She was the only one to die there. The only one to stay. Thus, it is Jean's story, and even more my own family's story, that I must turn to as a young adult in Nebraska and later upstate New York when trying to understand my longing for Sawbill, my love of the place, and my desire for the location, in moments of upheaval and change, to serve as a touchstone for family, for life.

THE BOUNDARY WATERS

WHEN KEVIN AND I pull into the Brule Lake parking lot in June 2008, the gravel road, dark wooden bulletin board, and narrow path to a single outhouse feel as familiar to me as the driveway of my grandparent's old house in northern Minnesota. Though I haven't been to Brule Lake before, I have been to Sawbill, a few lakes west, and the similarities between them calm me as Kevin and I unstrap the canoe from the top of his Mazda and carry it to the shore. Thin lines of blue peek from the crevasses of the long, gray clouds. The wind throws a shadowed spray of water against our arms and legs. As we load our packs into the canoe, I wonder where Kevin has put the engagement ring—if he has it in his pack or is saving it for after the trip, when I will continue showing him all the places I love on the North Shore.

"Ready?" he says, the packs loaded, the car locked.

"Ready," I reply. We scoot the canoe into the water, where it bobs slightly. I climb in and take the seat at the front. Kevin pushes off, hesitant at first, so that his foot grazes the water during his final lunge. The canoe rocks from side to side. The full weight of the wind hits our faces.

"Keep to the shore," I yell, eyeing the map I have placed in a waterproof bag and tied to the bar in front of me. Small islands the size of pitchers' mounds jut out of the water, one or two pines swaying on the rock. The islands don't appear on the map. Too miniscule, perhaps. But their quaintness pleases me, and if the canoe weren't sliding so quickly toward their rocky outcrops, I would pause to take a picture.

We move our paddles to the left side of the canoe, paddling in unison. The water pulls on my paddle, my arms, my shoulders, my back. The wind howls through the pines and the birches as the water slaps against the canoe. I haven't paddled on a lake since my family's kayaking trip the summer before. For Kevin, it's been even longer.

"That's good!" I yell when we lurch within thirty feet of the shore. "Too close!" I call again as my paddle hits rock.

We paddle on the right side now, turning the canoe away from the line of trees. We paddle quick, rapid strokes. The wind slugs me on the side of the face. I squint at the map and then at the water in front of us. The broad, animal-like spine of a wave nears, followed by the dark abyss behind it. As the wave smacks the canoe from the side, my stomach clenches and drops in the crest and roll.

Oh God, I think, *we're going to capsize three hundred yards from the landing.* I recall my father's remarks when I told him about this trip. "Brule Lake?" he'd said, with that undertone in his voice that made me nervous—that undertone that made me ask what was wrong with the lake. He said something about "big" and "east to west" and "waves" and perhaps even "boy scouts capsizing." "We'll be fine," I had answered. "Kevin's an Eagle Scout." I did not tell him that we had tried to get a permit for Sawbill Lake but that the Department of Natural Resources had sold out. I did not tell him that I wanted what my brother had: Boy Scout trips with my father, where ten-year-olds jumped off of cliffs near where my dad had grown up. I did not tell him that, when Kevin and I had discussed locations for a weeklong camping trip, the choice had been obvious. Kevin and I were talking about marriage. I wanted to show him the North Shore, and we'd figured that, if we survived a week in the Boundary Waters, we'd be good for life.

No, I had let the silence linger as it does now, as Kevin and I maneuver between a long, thin island and a cliff of granite and basalt. The wind moans above the birch and white spruce. The waves slap against the canoe and the rock, but in this channel they round at the top—less sharp and frothy.

"Just go straight," I tell Kevin, suddenly aware of how useless I feel.

The task proves impossible.

On Brule Lake, the second largest in the Boundary Waters, we learn we can't paddle in a straight line.

When my father, a scraggly teenager in cut-off jeans, lived on Sawbill Lake with my grandparents, the Boundary Waters Canoe Area was less than a decade old. Created by the Wilderness Act in 1964 and further protected by the Boundary Waters Canoe Area Wilderness Act of 1978, the watery region bordering Canada was quickly becoming one of the most visited wilderness areas in the United States. Already, outdoor enthusiasts from across the United States began portaging from lake to lake, pushing themselves on fourteen-day solo trips, or reveling in small groups as they explored a terrain equally comprised of islands and water. It was an area of connection, of fine distinctions, where Kevin's aunt once crossed into Canada without realizing it. A place where, I like to think, my father crossed into adulthood.

As the US Forest Service started banning motorboats from the area's outlying lakes, including Sawbill and Brule, my father perfected his canoe stroke, his fish filleting. He guided visitors around the rapids that separated lakes and sometimes took day trips by himself. Years later, on family backpacking trips and hikes near Brule, he'd name the lakes with an ease that buoyed me: here, an album of my family's history, kept safe on waterproof maps.

Yet, as Kevin and I pull, breathless, into an empty campsite on the north side of the lake, I cannot imitate my father's assuredness. We set up the tent in silence, and our lunch of peanut butter and honey tortillas sticks in my throat.

"We should probably practice," I say after eating. The wind has died down, and though the sky still sags with dark clouds, white caps no longer pock this part of the bay. We paddle in circles around the small inlet near our site, struggling to go straight. Kevin attempts to twist his paddle away from the canoe at the end of his stroke; I try to reach farther away from the canoe when I begin mine.

"You're not doing it right!" I chide when we again turn to the right, the dead pine we had decided to head for now drifting from my direct line of sight.

"I can't help it!" he says. He lifts his hat off his head and wipes his forehead with the sleeve of his shirt. The tight curls in his hair have already started to flatten. "I'm trying! Tell me, what exactly am I supposed to do?"

I slouch in my seat, resting my paddle on the gunnels. I lean into the back of my life jacket, stretching my spine. "Switch sides more often," I say, guiltily aware of the annoyance in my voice. "It's not my fault your strokes are more powerful."

We keep practicing, circling the inlet again and again. The bow of the canoe skims the water. A hawk glides overhead. When we get too close to the shore, Kevin performs what he calls an "Oh-Shit Stroke," pushing backwards so we slow and turn from the bank.

After an hour, we decide to paddle west, out of the inlet. Immediately, the surface of the lake begins to undulate as water unhindered for five miles by islands or land funnels into North Bay. The wind smothers me. I lower my head, forcing air in through my nose and out through my lips in a silent whistle. The waves come toward us again and again. I try to paddle in a steady rhythm, switching sides every ten strokes. I try to switch quickly—to keep the canoe from turning to the right or left as Kevin paddles solo. My arms ache but still we fumble in the open, vulnerable and weak. Still the waves come and the wind heaves against us, the paddle nearly useless in my hands.

"We're turning!" I yell into the wind. "We need to stay straight!"

I know Kevin is scowling, and it angers me—his inadequacy. I expected him to be more adept, but he is not. *We* are not.

I look back. He slouches on his seat, unwraps an energy bar he's taken from his pocket. "I'm going low," he says. Sweat glazes his forehead. His hands shake as he tears the wrapper.

I envision the canoe capsizing. I envision us bobbing in the roll of the water, pulling the canoe to an island or shore, where we slip on the wet rock and cut our legs. Kevin would go into a diabetic coma. The canoe would sink, and we'd be stranded; or it would hit us on the head as we floundered. We'd lose consciousness and drown and no one would know for a week.

We make our way into the bay where the waves lessen. Dead limbs bob at the mouth of a creek. A bent birch tree dips its leaves into the lake. I can tell from the shimmers in the distance where the waves are rougher—the glassy sheen where the water is calm.

"How are you doing?" I ask, looking back.

"Okay," Kevin says.

"We'll get better. We just need more practice," I say, though I am thinking about failure. I'm thinking: by the end of this trip, we'll probably break up.

"Yep," he answers, making his lips pop on the "p."

We let ourselves bob for a few minutes. I dangle my fingers into the water.

A man canoeing solo paddles past, a fishing line trailing from the stern. He paddles with the ease I saw in my father last summer: a deftness with the wooden handle, the quick lift from side to side. I lay my hand over the water so that it just touches the lake, then I lift my hand to let the water drop from my fingers.

When a breeze picks up, chilling my neck, we decide to start paddling back.

It's not yet six when we return to the campsite, but the cool shadows of trees hint at dusk. We pull on sweatshirts and change into dry sandals. We unload the small propane stove, tighten the nozzles, and start to heat water for our dehydrated supper. The propane hisses as it burns—a hiss so loud I'm sure anyone paddling near will hear it. Every once in a while the propane stove whines and spits. Kevin taps the cylindrical tank with his finger and it stops, but I step backward, worried that the stove is faulty and we'll soon blow up.

Once the water begins to boil, we open one of the two black bear canisters with the side of Kevin's car key and unpack the dehydrated red beans and rice. We'd stopped at REI on the drive up, like my family had always done before backpacking trips. I'd shown Kevin the racks of dehydrated meals, pointed out those my siblings and I did and didn't like. Now, I take over my father's role. I pull at the notched indent on the side and rip off the thin strip of plastic. I set the pouch on the ground and reach for the brown measuring cup.

"Want me to hold it?" Kevin asks.

"Sure," I say. I dip the cup into the pan of water and bring it to the bag. Kevin pinches the top open and lifts the pouch off of the ground.

As I tip the cup and start pouring, a few drops of water hit the edge of the bag and dribble onto the forest floor. A few more drops hit Kevin's hand, and as I tilt the cup, the drops become a stream—a stream of boiling water pouring down his fingers instead of falling into the bag.

"Ah! Son of a . . . " Kevin yells, dropping the bag, which lands on its side. Hard grains of rice and shriveled beans spill across the dirt, along with a watery soup of orange spices.

"Don't just stand there. Put your hand in the lake," I say, holding the now-empty cup.

Kevin crouches near the lake, his hand submerged to his wrist. As the broth of spices soaks into the ground, I remember the video the DNR officer had made us watch when we picked up our permit— the part where a bear paws at someone's discarded fish carcasses. The white letters on the screen reminded us to pack everything out— not to leave leftover food or fish carcasses in the brush.

I start picking up the grains of rice and putting them back in the bag. I scoop at a pile of beans with a spoon, pulling out a small twig. The water in the bag has begun to soften what didn't spill, the air suddenly spiced with cumin and pepper. Although we've brought enough food for one extra day, I do not intend to waste our first meal. I salvage as much as I can from the ground, and this time, the bag propped against a rock, I fill it with the required water, sealing it shut. I scoop the rest of the rice into the black garbage sack the DNR office provided.

Twenty minutes later, we sit on a log near the fire pit, the bag between us. Some of the beans are still hard, and every once in a while there's the taste of sage or twig. Kevin grimaces and plucks a pebble from his mouth. He throws it into the brush, scowling, before scooping out another small spoonful.

"It's not so bad, just roughage, right?" I say, though neither of us laughs, and by the final fourth of the bag even I'm not trying to make a light joke. Each spoonful of rice includes a fine grit of dirt—a sap-like curl of the tongue, a grating against the teeth. Bits of rice float in the brown broth; dirt clings to the side of the bag. I pull out a pine needle and hold it in front of me, dropping it into the garbage. I stare back into the pouch but don't move my spoon toward the opening. I set the spoon down.

This is not the trip I had expected. This is not like my family's backpacking trips. On those trips, I hiked with confidence from the backpacking trails into the state parks. My brother walked in front of me, my sister and parents behind. Sometimes I couldn't see anyone. I counted my footsteps and watched the ground and listened to the rustle of the leaves, the squirrels jumping in the trees. I passed couples with daypacks or water bottles strapped around their waists. I passed a family trekking along the trails for just a few hours. As we neared the park headquarters, the foot traffic increased. I was in middle school. I nodded to the people I passed, my backpack tugging at my shoulders, my hips. With my mud-crusted calves and sweaty bandana, I felt older. Rougher.

At Gooseberry Falls, small kids gawked at us as we swung our backpacks onto our knees and leaned them against the visitor's center. Tourists streamed from the RV-filled parking lot to the paths that led to the falls, elbowed each other in the gift shop, and pointed at the stuffed wolf on display. My family sat on the sidewalk next to the building, flapping the backs of our shirts so the sweat would dry. Heat simmered under the wood shingles, fragrant with beeswax.

I was proud. Proud of the overlooks we hiked to. Proud of Lake Superior, always a blue line against the horizon. I was even proud of the brown toilet pits off of thin trails in the woods. They never stunk of real outhouses, and the breeze dappled the shadows on my thighs.

There was an ease to those trips. I'd often wake before my

father, unzip the tent door and stumble into my shoes. I'd sit on the picnic table, or on a log near the fire pit, and read—read until the light eased the shadows from the trees and my father woke up to start heating water for breakfast.

Not like now. Now I seal the bag containing the rest of the red beans and rice. I put it into the garbage and lean on my elbows. I think of the long, choppy stretch of water we'll have to cross to get back to the car. I think of all those waves, waves like tiny roller coasters and the bile rolling in my gut.

Six miles away, on the westernmost edge of the lake, wind forces the trees to sway. I look up at the still leaves and listen to the distant sshhhhh—a sound that intensifies now, moving closer. Somewhere above us, an air mass we cannot see trucks eastward. The shrill grows until it rushes upon us—a surge and swirl in the leaves above. A few small branches and pine needles plop onto the fly of the tent. I pull my palms into the cuffs of my sweatshirt.

On the third day of our trip, Kevin and I sleep bundled in mummy sacks until the rising sun turns our tent into a sauna. In canoe time, it is late. We heat water for instant cappuccinos and carry them to the shore. The man we saw fishing two days earlier paddles to the west. Two canoes, one with a man, one with a woman, paddle east toward the bay. They paddle closer to our site than the man did. Their talk echoes across the water. When they spot us in our chairs, their voices soften. They do not zigzag.

"Do you want to head out on the water?" I ask, eyeing the couple.

"That's okay. I'm fine doing this," Kevin says.

I pick at the dirt beneath my fingernails and massage my palm. Dew drips from our canoe paddles, which lean against a tree. I swallow a sudden sense of guilt. Maybe I'm not cut out for this. Unlike my father, maybe I'm not worthy of this landscape.

We read and write in the stillness, listening to the chickadees and finches, the wind and the ripples of water in our inlet. As the sun warms the air, I take off my rain jacket, then my sweatshirt, then the faded long-sleeved T-shirt I'm wearing over another T-shirt. A loon floats into our small bay. Kevin wants to take a picture, but it dives into the water and we cannot find it anymore.

"I'm glad we're here," he tells me, a hand on my knee.

I touch the burn on his thumb. "Me too."

Across the water, the white trunks of birch stand out like matchsticks or bones.

"You were mad at me out there, weren't you," Kevin says, and though I pretend to look away, I must nod and say yes.

He leans back in his chair, his hands clasped. He reaches for his shoulder and rubs at a knot that formed yesterday after the portage.

I shrug. "I expected you to be better," I say. Then, "I expected us to be better."

I am thinking of my family's backpacking trips—the way everything was perfect. The way my dad manned the stove while we played near the water. The way he always knew what he was doing. No one got burned. No one felt overexhausted. If only I could repeat those trips, like a how-to guide I could follow step by step.

Two loons call to themselves. Kevin asks what I'm thinking about. I don't answer.

Not everything about those family backpacking trips, of course, was perfect. I hated being forced to finish the dehydrated chili. I hated the blisters that my dad would cover with moleskin. The blisters always popped, the skin sticking to the socks I peeled off in the evenings. And I hated the rain that kept us in the tents playing endless games of Go Fish, the flashlight suspended from a net at the top of the tent. I hated my dad telling me we had three more miles to the next campsite when all I wanted to do was wade in a creek and skip rocks across the lakes we passed. Most of all, I hated restuffing my sleeping bag every morning of every day for a week, only to roll it out again seven hours later.

I move my chair closer to Kevin's and lean against his arm.

"Sorry," I say. "I've been . . ."

"Irritable?" He brushes a mosquito from my shoulder. "Well, I was mad too."

"At our paddling?"

"That. And, well, you."

He tells me about the way I've been talking to him—the way I've ordered him around. The way I've taken over the cooking and the fire starting, not leaving anything for him. He says he feels emasculated.

"But I've been here before. I know what to do," I say.

"But we're both learning," Kevin says. "We should learn together."

The waves lap against the rocks, sucking against the dirt and roots near the canoe landing. A water spider flits across the surface.

"Maybe we should leave," I say, wondering what my father would do.

"Leave early?"

"Or just stay at state parks and take day trips on smaller lakes."

Kevin nods. "That sounds good," he says.

Miles and miles of lakes and swamp stretch north and west of us, clear to the Canadian border and even beyond. The expanse of all that terrain, those interconnecting waterways unmarked by gravel roads, presses like the wind against my back. I sigh. Only on the edge, we've already given up.

The string of state parks that Kevin and I head to after leaving the Boundary Waters act as a transition zone of their own—an entry and exit stop for canoeists and backpackers, as well as a rustic alternative to the motels and small resorts that stretch from Duluth to Grand Marais. Here, thin paths lead to overlooks of Lake Superior, spring runoff the color of root beer soars down the many waterfalls, and children search for agates at picnic areas near the lake. At Cascade River State Park, where we camp after Brule Lake, I breathe deeply and hold the cool air in my lungs. We are next to Lake Superior again, at a campground with running water. My family often stopped here after backpacking trips, and without expecting to, I recognize the layout of the trails.

"We can get to the falls this way," I say after we've once again set up our tent.

The campground's loops unfold before us—the paths and sites my siblings and I wandered, sizing up our backpacking tents against pop-up trailers—and for a while Kevin and I meander in silence. Pine needles soften the path. Children call from a play-ground nearby. Everywhere, towels drape on clotheslines, families rustle through coolers, and voices murmur from beneath rain flies and tarps. I reach for Kevin's hand, only to grasp air. When I turn, he is looking behind us and patting his pocket.

He must have the engagement ring. The realization travels like a spark up my spine. My mouth fills with the gritty taste of our botched rice and beans, and my hands burn from our failed pad-dling. I take the lead and walk quicker.

"It's beautiful here, isn't it," I say, not looking back to see his expression.

The clanking of pots and murmur of children recede and soften as we hike away from the campground. We follow the path along-side the river, cross a wooden bridge, and then begin hiking the other way down.

"Where's the waterfall?" Kevin asks.

"I don't know. A little farther." I swallow, wipe my hands on my shorts.

My parents got engaged by a waterfall at Gooseberry Falls, just twenty miles from here. They'd walked to the falls furthest from the visitor's center, sat at a bench and had a picnic lunch. Then my father had kneeled on the ground and proposed. There are pictures of my parents on the bench. My mother in a white polo, sitting sideways, her hands around her knees, the ring on her finger. Another of my father, alone and grinning. When I was in middle school and they'd taken us to Gooseberry Falls on one of our camping trips, my siblings and I had made them show us that bench. We took a family picture there, then one of just my parents. The brush had grown to conceal the falls, but the air still rung from the roar. And so my parents had smiled for us, our fingers clunky on the camera, my mother's hair cut now to her chin, my father's belly a little wider.

A family passes Kevin and me. The Cascade River begins to swirl and thunder. All week I've wanted to repeat the trips I took with my family. But now that we near the falls, the similarities between this trip and my parents' engagement prick at my neck like so many black flies.

"Go over there. I'll take your picture," Kevin says.

I swat at the flies in the air. Centuries of runoff have smoothed the red rock of the river's edge. I walk off of the path, make my way across pockets and dips where larvae now swim. I sit on a ledge and lean back, braced by my hands. The sun glints and I can't see Kevin's face, just the flash of the camera's red light. He motions me over, but I turn to the waterfall, watch the spray and the swirl at the bottom, the way foam floats toward the edge, toward the rock.

"What are you doing?" he yells, his voice muffled by the roar so that I could have ignored him if I really wanted to.

"Just looking," I yell back.

A woman with her dog passes on the bridge. Kevin pets the dog, who leans against his leg.

My family had played here on those childhood trips. We'd walked across this very bridge, even waded in the water. We'd propped our backpacks against the railing, unlaced our boots, pulled off our socks. My dad had fallen asleep on the bench over there, while my mom wiped her neck with a bandana. And now I am here with Kevin, and he is waiting for me with his camera, his pocket, his ring. I hug my legs, rest my cheek on my knee. When Kevin starts to walk toward me, I stand up.

"Hey," he says.

"Hey," I say, smiling.

"Where are you going?"

"Back to the bridge."

"But I just came over here."

"But now I'm done. Here. Let me take your picture."

He poses on the rock, the tips of his boots near one of the pools. He rests his thumbs in a belt loop. After I take the picture he starts walking back.

I lean against the railing, into the spray. A few hikers pass us. I don't look at them. Kevin walks up to my side, lets his elbow and shoulder touch mine. He glances around, watching for more hikers. He pulls at his palms.

I swallow, suck in my stomach, hold my breath.

"Hey," he says.

"Hey." And whether I want him to or not, he begins.

"I know we'll be apart for the next few years. I know it will be hard, but I also know we'll make it work," he says. "I've always known we'll make it work."

And he's talking now about how we'll make it work, about the way that he loves me, and I glance at his face, his cheeks red, the skin smooth, those curly whiskers on his beard, his blue eyes that stare at me, so vulnerable I must look away, back at the water that falls from the rock into the pool, where it foams and floats against more rock, kneaded by water for so long that minnows flit through slick pools.

Twigs snap. I hold my breath, catch my breath, but it's no one.

Just Kevin, who is saying all the right words, about marriage being hard, about marriage being a commitment but a commitment he knows he can make. And those words warp in the mist. They crash into the water. What did my father say to my mother twenty-four years ago? They were so young.

Yet I am young too, standing here in front of a waterfall, hovering almost, while Kevin talks. His mouth moves as my parents' image wavers to my left: my dad asleep on the bench, my mother with her wet bandana, and a few decades beforehand the two of them walking hand in hand. Another twig snaps. Voices move up the trail. I don't want an audience, can't have an audience. Kevin better not kneel, but he's in his pocket now, he's fingering something. The tendons in his knee relax and stretch as he moves down an inch.

"Stop," I say. "Just stop." And he stares at me. Stares. His mouth half-open, moving without forming words.

"I think it's time to go back." I turn and walk toward the campground. I move quickly, my strides long and tight. I listen for his footsteps behind me.

Back at the campsite, Kevin asks what I thought he was going to say. His eyebrows furrow, his eyes wet near the edges.

I stare at the fire pit, push a large stone with my foot.

"What did you think I was going to say?" he asks again.

"You know," I tell him, standing now on top of that stone, balancing over the ash in the fire pit. "What do you want to do now?" I ask.

He sits on the bench of the picnic table, rubs at his hands. He shrinks, his shoulders hunched, and I suddenly flush at what I have done. The confusion I've caused him. I bite my tongue, step down from the rock I'm still standing on. But I can't walk over.

Instead, I take out my pocketknife, use the can opener to turn the locks on the bear canister. I pull out the bag of trail mix. I toss it onto the table so that it lands with a splat, the peanuts and raisins and sesame sticks and M&Ms spreading out into a giant oval.

"Want to play a game?" I ask, my voice rough on the edges as if it clawed its way out of my throat.

"I guess."

We pull out the cribbage board, set out the pieces. Families in the campsites around us have started to make dinner, to prepare campfires for hotdogs and hamburgers. I shuffle the cards. Smoke rises from fire pits around us, hangs in the air. The doors to the bathrooms across the campground clang shut again and again. We mutter numbers, forget to count points.

Goosebumps run up my arms. My knees bang against each other. I hold them together, tight, and pull on a rain jacket to use as a windbreak. I realize I am scared.

"Why did you stop me?" Kevin asks again.

I pick up a card. Discard. A bird calls—a high song I always hear up here and have come to love, though I do not know the name of the bird.

"I don't know," I say.

Kevin places a card facedown on the pile, shows me his winning hand. I collect the cards and deal again.

"What did you think I was going to do?"

"You know." I sigh. "I just wasn't ready. Not to be proposed to like that."

"Like what?"

"Like that. By a waterfall. With you on your knees." I do not add that it felt too close to the way my parents got engaged: the bench at Gooseberry Falls. Our images suddenly superimposed on theirs in a way I expected to comfort me but instead found disquieting.

"But I thought you were ready. We've talked about it. I thought it would be romantic."

"I know." I take a card from the draw pile, lay it on the discard pile so that the plastic slaps. We continue playing in silence. A couple walks past, tells us good evening. We both smile through tight lips, nod and return their greeting.

"I just wasn't ready to be proposed to," I say. "I'd rather it be mutual. A discussion."

"Ok."

"It was just too formal."

He frowns, his eyes shadowed by his heavy brow. "Well then. How do you feel about marriage?"

"I don't want to get married yet."

"So you don't want to get engaged?"

"That's not what I said."

"What then."

"I'm just not ready to get married."

"Well neither am I."

I look at him. At his nose, which is slightly too big, the curls on his head, the fleshy earlobes I like to pull. The way he wears emotions on his face, so easy to read, the way he honors how he feels instead of always trying to hide it like me, so contained I can hardly admit to my own fear. He will be good to me. He will be loyal.

"We need some stipulations," I say. "I don't want to get married until we've both finished our master's programs. And one of us needs to have a solid job."

"I would agree," he says. "If you hadn't stopped me, I would have said the same thing."

I smile.

"So, are we engaged?"

"Show me the ring."

He pulls out a small black box and opens it to reveal a silver band with nine tiny inset stones. It's flat on top, technically an anniversary ring, because he knows I didn't want anything that would stick out.

"You can put it on me," I tell him. "Just don't get on your knees."

He slips it onto my finger, where it hangs, cold against my skin. "Will you marry me?" he says.

"Eventually." I flex and unflex my hand. I set it over his hand. Then I draw another card from the pile and we return to our game.

We spend two more days along the North Shore. We stay at the state park and take day trips to Grand Marais. I smile at Kevin, hold his hand when no one else is around, and sometimes when others are around. I try to get used to the weight of the ring, to its existence there. I like the authority it gives me when we buy wood from the camp office. I feel legitimate—we are not just some teenagers on a rendezvous. But I haven't told my parents, and at night, after Kevin has fallen asleep, I listen to the hoot of the owls, to the whispers of other campers across the park. I am scared. Scared this won't last. Scared that I am no longer a child. Scared that my life has split from my parents' and I can no longer pretend to control the future. After this trip, Kevin will return to his job in Milwaukee, I will return to Mankato, and eventually, at the end of the summer, we will each move again to Michigan and Nebraska for graduate school. I tell myself that, if we are meant to be together, it will work out. If we aren't, we'll learn quickly. The wind picks up. Pine needles drop onto our tent with small pings. I readjust my sweatshirt and small camp pillow, but it takes a long time to fall asleep.

The next day we drive a few miles south to Gooseberry Falls State Park, where, less than thirty years before, my father proposed. We walk through the packed parking lot to the visitor's center and then meander around the more popular waterfalls. Families with children and grandparents in wheelchairs crowd the railings. A fine mist of spray hugs the rocky cascades. We opt for the more strenuous dirt path that will lead us to the high falls. As we hike, the crowds thin.

"I'll show you the bench where my parents got engaged," I tell Kevin.

The path skirts the river, moving toward and away from it as we climb, so that sometimes the river clamors and sometimes it murmurs. The ground sinks beneath us; the air buzzes with mosquitoes. I keep glancing at my map, wondering how much farther we have until the high falls, the bench. When we finally get there, I almost fail to notice it. Brush has overgrown the less-used path, obscuring the overlook under a damp shadow.

"Here it is," I say, pointing. I walk around the bench, wipe wet leaves from the wooden surface.

We sit on it together. We look through the alder to the water below, to the hiss of the falls.

"I feel like I should propose again," Kevin says.

He jiggles a leg, kneads his hands, and then clamps them between his knees.

"You can if you feel like it," I say.

A squirrel leaps between two trees and a single leaf slips to the ground.

"I guess not," Kevin says. "It's too late. Should we take a picture though? Of us here, like your parents?"

I shake my head. "No. That's okay."

My mother had just turned nineteen when they got engaged, yet in photographs of them on the bench, she looks older—her faint smile, the popped collar of her polo shirt, the permed hair. Even my father looks older than his twenty-three years. His hairline already starting to recede, his body solid as if he knows what he's doing. We are older than they were, here in the same place. Though maybe they, too, felt uncertain. Maybe they, too, hesitated before a future they couldn't predict: the upcoming birth of my brother, followed closely by me. The job changes and illnesses. The moves from one state to another. If, in coming to the Boundary Waters, I expected the safety of the familiar to ensure how my own story might progress, I was misled.

Kevin presses his thigh against mine and I shiver. "Ready?" I say. Touching this same bench, looking at the same waterfall, I feel I'm stepping into my parents' story, and I know now that I can't. It's not mine to touch.

BIKING BEHIND DAD

🦋 MY OWN STORY of the North Shore, though different from my father's, is nonetheless about him. It is about camping and canoeing and a teenager's need to connect. Which is why, the summer after my freshman year of college, I find myself, with some hesitation, pulling my bicycle out of the garage and mounting it behind him, ready to train for a weeklong ride that will return us to the northwoods. It is early May. Small nubs of leaves protrude from the trees and the air smells of mud. The tires of my bike vibrate against the asphalt as my dad and I swish past the single-family neighborhoods, along a cornfield, and then down the Mount Kato hill, where the bare ski slopes now show the faint hatching of mountain bike paths. As we curve down and into the Minnesota River valley in south central Minnesota, I hover over the brakes, not sure whether to slow down. Leftover grit from snow plows spits from my tires. When the two-mile climb to the end of the trail begins, my dad, who has biked behind me, speeds past my left. I pedal to keep up. Beads of sweat slide down my forehead, along my nose and cheeks, eventually hitting my lips. I taste the salt.

With a mile and a half to go, my dad manages to keep a constant pace while I fall farther behind. My legs ache and my throat grows thick. For years, my father dreamt of biking the National Multiple Sclerosis Society's The Ride Across Minnesota, a three-hundred-mile, five-day fundraising trek affectionately called the MS TRAM. Each spring he'd tune his bike, spend a Saturday afternoon oiling the gears, and buy new batteries for the lights. I never knew why he wanted to go. I figured it was like all his other dreams: to move to Alaska, to own a yacht, to hike the Appalachian Trail—dreams he'd share after returning from business trips or during the commercials between episodes of Star Trek. "Next year," he'd say. "Next year." But next year would come, the newspapers would print photographs of bicyclists congregating in cornfields, and my father would slump in the recliner, too busy with work, an arm draped to block the light from his eyes.

That winter, when I'd learned the TRAM would be held in northeastern Minnesota, with a final stretch along Lake Superior, I'd told my dad I'd go with him. I'd spent mornings and weekends on the stationary bike in my dorm's basement, sending an e-mail after to tell him how many miles I'd biked. But now, as I stare at the asphalt and try to concentrate on the trail, on the repetitive motion of the pedals, I can't help but clench my jaw.

"How are you doing?" he calls back.

"Fine," I manage to croak, but I am thinking of inadequacy: the tennis matches he missed when I was in high school, the brief conversations we'd had the past year while I was in college: *How was your day? Fine. Yours? Fine. How is school? Busy. How is work? Lots of grading. Sounds like fun. Indeed.* As my dad's brown bike pulls farther ahead, my entire summer deflates . . . the return to the North Shore, to the pine tree and birch, where my dad isn't staring at computer screens but at the stars and the woods. We haven't been up there for more than four years.

My dad pedals ahead, out of sight past a bend. I stand on my own pedals, using gravity to help me make it up the final stretch. At the top, where my dad waits, I hold my breath against a gasp. "I'm not used to those hills," I say, slapping on a smile.

"That's why we're training," my dad says, straddling his bike. "Just keep biking. Soon you'll get up the hills without a problem."

I reach for my bottle. Water dribbles down my chin, onto my shirt. I wipe at it with my hands.

"Ready to head back?" he asks. The transition lenses of his glasses darken his eyes. His own bottle stays clamped to his bike.

"I guess," I say.

And so we train. All summer, we bike at least eleven miles five days a week. I learn the route to Rapidan well: through the cornfield, past Mount Kato, down the hill into the river valley, along the woods, under the highway, past the farm that smells of sewage, around the bend to the five-mile marker, under three wooden bridges, and finally back up into cornfields, where we turn around at the gravel road and head home. Some nights I work at the nursing home until seven, get home, eat a light dinner, and then go biking with my dad. The sky darkens the last few miles, the shadows of trees turning the woods to night. We bike faster, trying to outpace the sunset, arriving at home to find dozens of gnats plastered against our necks.

Then we increase the distance of our rides. We no longer ride eleven miles, but thirty, with sixty-mile rides on the weekends. Our rides become the planning point for our days. I learn to discuss the TRAM when I don't know what to say to my dad. I ask him about the mileage. He asks if I need anything for my bike. I ask him if he is sore since we biked forty-five miles yesterday instead of a mere thirty. Before I go to bed, I stop by my dad's office, where he stares into three computer screens, papers and student essays spread out on his desk.

"Hey dad," I say from the doorway, wary of interrupting.

"Hey," he replies.

I step inside and spin around in the extra swivel chair that sits next to the desk my mother sometimes uses. "When do you want to bike tomorrow?"

"Well, when do you work?"

"Eleven to two and then three to seven."

He frowns, finishes typing an e-mail, and touches a hand to his chin. "Well, we should probably do an early one tomorrow then. I have to be at work at ten."

"Ok. When do you want to start?"

"How early are you willing to wake up?"

"Not *too* early," I say, swiveling back and forth in the chair. "I can probably handle 7:00 a.m. again though."

"That would be fine."

"Ok." I stand from the chair.

"See you in the morning."

But by the morning, when my radio alarm goes off, I grope for the snooze button and must will myself to leave the warm sheets. A toilet flushes somewhere in the house, and heavy footsteps move from the front door to the kitchen. I place my feet on the cool floor, using my toes to feel for the bike shorts near my hamper. I put the shorts on in the dark so that I don't wake my sister. I dig through my hamper, smelling each athletic shirt until I find one that isn't too rank. My hair sticks up on one side and my eyes struggle to focus. I wonder what would happen if I skipped a day—if I didn't show up and stayed in bed. I pull a clean pair of socks from my dresser drawer and head downstairs.

"Good morning," my dad says from the kitchen table with a cup of coffee and the newspaper.

I grab a granola bar from the cupboard and reach for the comics. We sit in silence, reading and eating, trying to wake up.

"Well," he says, setting down the paper. "Are you ready?" His eyes are red like mine, puffy and tired at the corners.

"I suppose," I say. I put on my shoes and head into the garage, swallowing the anxiety I always feel right before a ride. When I straddle my bike, the thin padding of the seat presses against still-sore muscles. I adjust my posture and position, but the ache remains.

Without many words, we begin riding. The morning air hits my face. I shiver, squinting and then opening my eyes wide. On the bike path, we dodge the sticks that have fallen overnight and the chipmunks that race in front of our tires. I breathe deep.

"I can't seem to wake up this morning," I say.

"Me either. I stayed up much too late last night," my dad says behind me, his pedaling rhythmic and clear.

"I'm glad it's so nice out though."

"Yes. I hope that the TRAM is like this."

We fall back to silence, biking a little longer. Only a few other joggers and bikers are out on the trail. I search my mind, trying to think of something to discuss with Dad. I ask him how his summer classes are going and he tells me about his problem students. I tell him about some of the residents at my job at the nursing home—the old man who has a crush on me or the lady who only eats peanut butter sandwiches and French fries. He teases me about the hills—hills I am afraid of. I see the great round mound of earth in front me, the small curve of a road heading up its belly, and my gut twinges. I worry I won't make it up, that I will embarrass myself and have to get off the bike. I worry that the exertion will be too hard, that I will fall behind. My dad rides beside me, urging me to keep the rhythm, to beat the hills.

"Say: I *love* those hills!" he yells, in an overly joyful voice I can't help but smile at.

I giggle, shake my head, and focus on pedaling.

"I can't hear you! I *love* those hills!" he calls again from behind and then suddenly from my side, where he grins, wide enough to show the gap between his two front teeth.

I smile, face forward, and push harder against the pedals. By the time we reach the top, we both breathe heavily.

"Now say it! Come on! I want to hear you!" he prods once more.

"Nope," I reply, "but I'm glad it's done today."

He laughs, soft, almost under his breath, and for a moment I laugh as well.

The days pass in a continuous cycle of working and biking until it's the end of July and time for the TRAM. We strap our bikes to the back of my dad's jeep and drive from Mankato to Duluth, where we will catch a shuttle to the starting line three hundred miles west. The familiarity of the drive eases the apprehension I have felt all summer—the endless training, the long hours alone with my dad. We pass gas stations we stopped at when I was younger; we climb hills I remember from our last backpacking trip, four years ago. The elm and oak change to pine in our silence. As Lake Superior spreads its tendrils across the horizon, I clasp my hands in my lap and squeeze tight. We have been here before.

At the starting point, we fill out the last of the paperwork and receive our T-shirts and bike numbers. Throngs of bikers move about in the giant parking lot. They greet each other as if at a family reunion, looking over their bikes one last time before the ride begins tomorrow, joking in groups of three or five while eating spaghetti from one of the food booths. I gaze, wide-eyed, at the multicolored bike shirts, the limber, long-legged throngs. My father's face shines like my own. That night neither of us sleeps.

We arrive at the grounds the next morning at seven. I eat my pancakes quickly, tapping my feet against the cement floor of the picnic shelter, ready to get on the trail and join the other bikers already pedaling away. "Ready?" I say. "Ready," my dad replies.

The route meanders through the pine forests, skirting along the edges of iron pits, their red slopes dipping into water that seems bluer than our lakes at home. My dad and I climb hills and go down hills, the excitement carrying us quickly along the trail. We don't talk, and I don't feel the need to initiate any conversation. The event and the crowds engross us. Our muscles are well developed with the training—they move on their own—and I find that we can keep up with and even pass some of the other bikers, everyone decked out in matching wristbands and padded biking shorts. "On your left," I say, as my dad and I pass a couple riding a tandem bike. We swish through the forests and little towns, part of the long, scattered line of thirteen hundred bikers, everyone waving to the townsfolk who watch our parade.

My dad and I reach the end of the route between noon and two every day, wobbling off of our bikes after accomplishing the fifty-five to seventy-two miles in five- to six- hours. Black flies litter the front of our shirts and we quiver as we walk, but we have completed the day's ride. We laugh at people we have met and hills we mastered. Like those evenings after a long hike, once we'd put up the tent and heated water for dinner, I feel close to my dad—to everyone biking the TRAM. While waiting in line for the bathrooms and food tents, we discuss the ride with strangers we have never spoken to before.

"How was your ride today?" one man asks another.

"Great! But boy, those headwinds on Country Road 34!"

"Oh, I know!" another girl joins in. "I actually had to downshift in order to go down that hill!"

My dad and I glance at each other, recalling how we'd leaned over our handlebars and panted during that stretch of road as well.

On Tuesday afternoon, just as we finish that day's route, it begins to rain. Not wanting to be stuck in our tent all evening, we put on our raincoats and bike to Hibbing's small sandstone public library. The rainwater coats my legs with grit and sprays onto my back as we pedal through the puddles and park our bikes in the racks in front of the building. Cool drafts of air seep in through the open windows of the library's two main rooms. As the sweat and rainwater on my arms, legs, and back begins to dry, I shiver. My dad quickly stakes out a table and opens his laptop to check his e-mail while I find a small chair in the corner of the library. I wipe dust from its arms and blow dead beetles from the window ledge behind it. Across the room, my dad hunches over his laptop, his fingers as quick as the rain splattering the windows. I open my journal and smile at him, but he doesn't look at me.

That evening, we stop at the corner drugstore and purchase a cribbage board. The rain continues to tap against our tent as we unroll our sleeping bags and prepare for a tournament—the first cribbage game we will have played against each other in years. We deal hand after hand until the sun starts to set and it grows too dark to see the cards. Outside of our tent other bikers stumble around rain flies and tent stakes, unzipping their raincoats as they prepare for the night. Their voices and whispers ease into the drizzling rain and the darkness. I close my eyes, let my bones and sore muscles sink into the damp ground. Tomorrow we will wake up and ride again. We will stand slowly, straddle our bikes, pedal along the asphalt and gravel roads, through the Superior National Forest we so often visited when I was younger. There, more than anywhere else—surrounded by those trees, by those paths—my place on this earth and my relationship with my dad will feel right and familiar and perfect.

Friday rolls around all too quickly. My bag of dirty clothing smells horrible, my butt is too numb to hurt, and my thigh muscles ache whenever I stand up after sitting down. Yet I do not want the week to end.

The last day's route—a mere twenty-six miles from Two Harbors to Duluth—takes us along the old Highway 61. To our left, alder and birch slope toward the red rock of Lake Superior's shore. To our right, gravel driveways lead to small cabins and old-fashioned resorts, then up to the wooded hills and valleys. Hand-painted signs advertise firewood and hand-parched Minnesota wild rice. Larger billboards show pictures of Gooseberry Falls and Split Rock Lighthouse. At a bend in the road, a peninsula of rock stretches into the lake, its fingertip thin and gray, covered with a faint mist. The waves crash again and again. The shadow of a barge speckles the horizon.

"What a view!" my dad says as we pedal along in our matching TRAM shirts. "I've forgotten how much I love it up here."

I think back to that stop at the Sawbill parking lot, when he'd stared into the trees. I want to hold this moment for him, capture it so that it repeats again and again, so that we are here, always, biking on these paths.

We continue quietly, comfortably, the long silences no longer a bother. I breathe in the pine and listen to the frigid water lap against the boulders of the shore. The pine trees thin, and in the distance Duluth's skyline appears like a haze. Traffic picks up—SUVs and trucks pulling canoes and motorized boats pass us, whipping grit against our helmets and sunglasses. I hear my dad's bike behind me, the consistent strumming of his gears, the sound I have been listening to constantly for five days, for the entire summer. As townhomes and condos begin to block our view of the shore, I feel the week slip away. I grip the handlebars of my bike and cough into the exhaust.

At the finish line, pedestrians lean against barricades, clapping their hands and cheering as each biker pedals past. They wave and blow horns, whistling as if we have just finished the Tour de France. I sit up straighter and slap the hand of an observer who holds it out for a high five. I wonder what my dad is thinking—if he's enjoying this moment. The cheering crowd obscures the thrum of his bike and his breath. I try to glance over my shoulder, to gauge his expression, but my bike skitters against loose gravel and the path narrows. I hope he is proud of us—of me.

The stream of bikers continues down a small hill, toward the lake and the rose garden. The cheers of the crowd soften, replaced again with wind and waves. At the bottom of the hill the path opens to a large meadow where hundreds of bikes lie on the grass. My legs wobble. Excitement lights my dad's expression—his eyes open, his smile wide with pride.

My dad digs around the small pouch strapped beneath his bike seat. He pulls out his camera and asks someone to take a picture of us. I stand beneath the large sign, smiling while I look at the camera, but before the woman snaps the picture, he interrupts her.

"Come closer," he says to me, gesturing with his fingers.

And I do.

We head back home later that day. At first the highway is filled with cars that have bikes strapped to their tops or backs. MS TRAM numbers flap against the bike frames; I feel connected to each one.

But as we near the Twin Cities, other cars and SUVs clog the interstate, and soon we note fewer and fewer bikes. I slump, slightly, as the North Shore's pine trees change into oaks and elms. It is over. It is actually over, and it will never happen again. I rub my thumb over the ridge of the medallion each participant received. Already I miss the North Shore. Already, as we drive away, I long for it, with the same longing I will feel years later, when my father moves from Minnesota.

There's an emptiness to my longing that I don't associate with me but with something larger. When we uproot ourselves, our memories are suddenly isolated. We carry them with us still, but they are not mirrored in the land we see around us: the kinds of clouds in the sky, the trees, and the dirt.

Taking those memories away from a place . . . what do they become? They become sad. Diminished. Their lifespan is shorter. They lose detail, becoming black-and-white profiles so grainy that, years later, I will sit down with the few physical reminders I have— photographs of the MS TRAM and of my family's backpacking trips and of Sawbill—and it won't be enough. I will worry about what I have and what I don't have and what richness of life my experiences and choices have deprived me of. To not see every fall and winter and spring and summer here, in this land that I love, in this land that my family has loved? To not feel wholly, entirely, every ounce of me—my skin cells and body chemistry and finger- nails and tears—as a reaction to and a part of this place . . .

It is a loss impossible to describe. But it thrums in my chest, and I have to believe, want to believe, that others feel it, too. That when packing boxes and saying goodbye to an environment that has given us memories and sustained us, even if we are moving because of something good—something we are excited about— that something else, something we can't quite describe but feel in our cells, in our fingertips, in our nostrils, is lessened because of it. That in uprooting ourselves, we always, always, leave something behind.

And so, as the North Shore slips farther behind us, and the number of bikes on the highway continue to thin, I reach out to my father to try and draw him in once again. "Was it worth it?" I ask, my voice high, still jubilated by the bike ride, by our time together there.

"Definitely," he replies. His hands rest on the top of the steering wheel. The sun makes the lenses of his glasses darken. "It was a long time coming, but it was worth it."

And I know he is right. Our conversation again falls into silence, but for the first time since I started high school and then college, the silence doesn't make me clamp my jaw. As we leave the North Shore and return to southern Minnesota, I realize that, here at least, perhaps our reticence doesn't mark all that is left unsaid but rather all that has been said and that doesn't need to be said. He does not need to say that he is glad we did this together, that our memories in this place are important, or that he loves me. After three hundred miles in these forests, along these lakes—after three hundred miles here, more than anywhere else—I just know.

SAWBILL MAP

🥨 WHEN KEVIN AND I move from the Midwest to upstate New York, the first—and for many months only—decoration we buy is a black poster frame from Target. The frame is a compromise. After living in different states for two years, we've grown stubborn about possessions. Kevin says his history books should go in the most prominent bookcase, his illustrations of 1700s military uniforms on the wall next to the desk. I insist that guests would prefer reading the titles of poetry and fiction and that he has claimed too much wall space in the office already.

"Something in this room needs to be mine," I say when I catch Kevin pounding in a nail for a Kandinsky imitation I painted and then gave to him during college, largely because he liked it and I hated it.

We stare at the empty wall above the roll-top desk Kevin inherited from his grandfather.

"How about the photographs we took at the Boundary Waters?" Kevin says.

"No. But maybe the watercolor of my grandma?"

Kevin scrunches his nose. "I'm sorry, but I don't really like that one."

"Why not?"

Kevin shrugs. "I just don't. Our diplomas?"

"No."

"Come on. They'd be perfect. Why not?"

"I don't care about those. They're just paper," I say. "I can't believe you don't like the watercolor of my grandma. It's my favorite painting."

"Jennie," Kevin sighs.

"What?" I sit on the floor, pull my legs to my chest and rest my chin on my knee. The floor is gritty from the boxes and unpacking. I wipe dirt from the bottoms of my feet. "What about a map," I say. "The map from the Boundary Waters."

Kevin studies the wall.

"It's large enough," I add. "It would probably look good there."

Kevin frowns, stares at the wood paneling our landlords have painted white. He starts to nod, then smiles. "Yes. I think it would."

And so we splurge. We are living off savings while Kevin looks for a job, minimizing errands to use as little gas as possible. The $26 for the extra-large black poster frame combined with the drive to Target feels luxurious. We take our time moving through the aisles, pausing in front of bathroom displays and shower curtains, vacuum cleaners and a programmable coffee maker to replace the one that fried in Kevin's storage unit before the move. After two hours we roll our nearly empty cart to the front of the store and chuckle when the cashier scans the frame and asks, "Is that all?"

But the frame pleases us. Back at the apartment, I tear the plastic wrapping from our purchase and pull the map from a desk drawer. Brule Lake, where we camped the summer we got engaged, sits massive in the northeast quadrant, peppered with red dots signifying campsites. Sawbill Lake, long and thin, trails down the southwest quadrant, only ten miles away as the crow flies.

"Are both lakes showing?" I ask after I've folded the map to fit the frame.

"Not quite," Kevin says.

I adjust the map and show it to him again.

"Perfect." He reaches for a nail and hammer.

Once we've hung the map, we stand back, admiring the way the creases show through the glass. We trace the route we drove, the portage to Echo Lake where we saw a moose, the landing where we'd discovered we'd left the car keys at the campsite. We look at Brule Lake and remember the waves, the discussions of marriage, the lap of water on shore. And I glance at Sawbill, note the parking lot I'd visited as a child, the memories I have there of my father, and am pleased I can see it, too—both lakes, in one view, as well as the meandering passageways and portages between them, those blue and red connections that have existed all along.

ANOTHER SWISS FAMILY ROBINSON

🦋 OUR SECOND FULL summer in upstate New York, I discover an old newspaper article about the Argobusts. The newspaper article, originally published on July 29, 1940, in the *Minneapolis Times Tribune*, is "twenty-ninth" in a series about "interesting Minnesotans," and the front page contains two large photographs of Jean and George. Jean stands next to a birch tree, a dappled forest behind her. She wears a striped shirt that puffs at the wrists, tucked just into a dark, empire waist skirt with large white buttons. She does not look at the camera but rather off to the left, past the fold in the newspaper. With her half smile, full face, high forehead and hair pulled back in the 1940s style, Jean fills the frame, sturdier and thicker in complexion than one would expect for someone on the front of the paper. She exudes a matronly confidence. She could knock me over if she wanted.

On the other side, in the top right, the blonde-haired George stares directly into the camera, smiling wide enough to show off his six top teeth. His brow slightly shadows his eyes. His short blonde hair cowlicks in the front, reminding me of some unnamable character actor, someone who laughs and drinks a little too much but not enough to become problematic.

"Another Swiss Family Robinson Hews Way Out of Depression in North Woods," the title of the article reads. Knowing what I do about Jean and George, I am surprised to be holding a love story.

> This is the story of a man and a woman who were licked to a frazzle by the Great Depression of '30 and '31.
>
> Nothing unusual about that, you may say, there were plenty more in the same boat. But there was something unusual about this pair, for while the collapse of their world knocked the wind out of them, with their second wind THEY licked the Depression. [. . .]
>
> Through sheer grit and stick-to-itiveness they carved out a new life for themselves in a totally new environment. Without money or backing or physical equipment; with nothing but high courage, in nine years they fought their way to a life happier and fuller of fundamental satisfaction than any they could have found if life had not given them that mighty punch below the belt.

And so begins the story of the Argobusts, a story I can hardly reconcile with what I have read from my other sources. I read with curiosity, with humor, as Vivian Thorp of the *Minneapolis Times Tribune* continues, in her heightened language, to describe the "stone broke" Argobusts immediately after George's wife's death and the way their lives eventually intersect with Jean's:

> Then one afternoon in Chicago something happened; just one of those trivial happenings which sometimes determine the fate of men and nations.
>
> The younger children had been off visiting a lady they had met and they liked her so much and she gave them such a happy time, that Argobust thought he should meet her, too.

She turned out to be younger than he expected, only in her middle twenties, but he liked her as his children had and the acquaintance grew. [. . .]

Then one day Wilson wrote his Father like this "Dad you're a big goop! What's the use of trying to buck this business game; there's nothing in it; you're just wearing yourself out. Give it up and come on up north and make a fresh start."

Said Argobust to himself, "I may be nutty, but why not."

He and the kids went over and talked to their new friend, Jean, and she too said "Why not?" Argobust said: "I'd like to have you go along." And once more Jean said, "Why not?" Said Argobust "Alright, let's get married." And Jean said simply "O.K."

"That," Thorp writes, "was how the partnership to lick the depression started."

According to Thorp, George called Jean "a hard-hitting sweetheart and the spark-plug of this whole enterprise." According to Thorp herself, Jean is "quite a gal." After describing Jean's history in hotel management and her gender-bending education, Thorp admits that Jean "had a dream; She wanted to run a resort of her own. Maybe when George Argobust made that extraordinary proposal, she glimpsed a remote possibility of making her dream come true in the north country."

In this, Thorp's description of Jean begins to mirror my own vision. Jean as a focused, determined woman, willing to do what she must to gain a livelihood and make use of her skills. As Thorp describes the rest of the adventure—the initial drive up to Tofte, the fight for funding, the summer the family camped out on the property, the process of cutting and prepping logs for the lodge— Jean remains a solid fixture.

"Jean didn't know what failure meant," Thorp says, and through

Thorp's frame, the family turns into smiling portraits of teenage children and men squatting with backpacks and canoe oars in front of log cabins, blankets around their necks, curls in their hair, and the sort of outdoorsy liveliness that has captured imaginations for so long.

"I've called this a team story," Thorp reflects, "and it was so in the main; but it was something more; it was also a sort of modern version of Swiss Family Robinson, for every one of those five children—six, with Toni, had a big part in it. Every one of them helped with enthusiasm, co-operation and hard work. Best of all, while that job was getting done a lot of fine character building was getting done also."

What Thorp doesn't mention—and in 1940 wouldn't have known—was that George and Jean would divorce during the Second World War. When peace treaties were signed and American families again began to visit summer resorts, it was Jean, not George, who would return to Sawbill. Jean and her future husband Dean Raiken define the Sawbill of the 1950s and 1960s. George, with his wide smile and blonde cowlick, disappears.

What would Vivian Thorp have said of this turn of events? Though I know she wrote to entertain—to provide a portrait of "interesting Minnesotans"—I cannot help but feel some sort of glee at all she gets wrong. The liveliness of her story—the sparkiness of Jean and George and all the children—bothers me:

"Why not?" they say to each other.
"You're a big goop!"
"O.K."

Their frazzled cheerfulness undermines the admiration I want them to take to the land. I want them to stand in front of Sawbill

Lake and see in it a quiet beauty that will haunt them the rest of their lives, even after Jean and George divorce and the children move to different states. I want them to obsess over Sawbill, like me—to give it the seriousness it deserves. Place as a way to preserve connections, to preserve memories and ways of being in the world, even if those connections later change.

Jean and the Argobusts didn't lick the depression. Rather, by coming to Sawbill, they let the lap of water on rocks strip them of their anger, their exhaustion, their many, many pretenses, until all that was left was Jean, who perhaps had nowhere else to go but who nonetheless came back.

I read Thorp's article again and again, appreciating its spunk, as well as its oversights. It makes me feel better about myself and what I try to get out of the family's history. I like thinking I know more about the Argobust family than Thorp did and that my image of them is somehow more complex and thus true.

But of course it isn't.

Thorp's depiction of Jean and the Argobusts is as flawed and imperfect as my own. In the end, we cannot know who they actually were or how they actually interacted. Even the Argobusts hide behind a scrim—their own oral histories colored by censorship and unspoken motives. Jane protects her father and speaks little of the divorce. No one else mentions it. Wilson writes of the resort's founding, but he says nothing of why he never returned. The "ideal partnership" that Thorp describes had a purpose and succeeded in the lodge's birth, but beyond that, Sawbill never became a utopia— for them, or, I begin to fear, for me. The successful marriage fell apart.

HOMEMAKING

KEVIN AND I promise ourselves that, after the wedding, we will buy furniture and paint. For the past few months in New York we've stored our clothing in cardboard boxes along the side of the bedroom. We've tripped over them in the night, scraped our legs on the paper flaps. "We don't have the money. Be patient," I tell Kevin whenever he complains about the apartment's white walls, the bare floors, the half-lived-in look of the boxes in the bedroom. His double mattress sags in the middle, and at night we roll into each other, wake up with one sweaty arm up against another's sweaty back.

But the emptiness of the walls bothers me, too. Mornings, I take my mug of coffee to the second bedroom-turned-office and stare at the window. I have no stories. I don't know what the view will look like in the winter—if we'll see the hills or the highway once the leaves fall, if trick-or-treaters will walk by on Halloween. I feel nothing for the corners of the walls, the scratch where some piece of furniture must have been pulled across the floor. I sit in my chair, holding my hands around the mug of coffee, and wait for the room to feel familiar.

After his shifts at Barnes and Noble, where he's found a part-time job, Kevin picks up paint swatches from Home Depot and Lowes. We carry the slips of paper around the apartment, hold them up to walls and windows. Greens and blues, yellows and browns, reds and burgundies.

"This one?"

"No."

"Maybe this one."

"I like this more."

We want the colors to brighten the rooms, to help us claim them as our own.

"I wish we could start now," Kevin says from the futon, where he's checking boxes on the back of the colors we like best.

"I know. But we will soon," I reply.

Less than a week after the wedding, Kevin calls me on his way home from work. It is 7:00 p.m. and Home Depot will be open until 9:00 p.m. "Want to pick up the paint?" he asks from his cell phone.

"Tonight?"

"Yeah. Tonight."

We plan to shop for mattresses and bedroom furniture once Kevin has a day off. But he wants to get the paint right away. "Besides," he says, "we should paint the rooms before we bring in any large furniture."

I change back into jeans from my sweatpants. When Kevin pulls into the driveway and walks up the flight of steps to the back door, he is grinning.

"How was work?" I ask.

"Eh," he says. His shirt smells of coffee and foamed milk. Splatter marks stain his shoes and pants. He changes into a long-sleeve T-shirt and jeans and pulls a Green Bay Packers cap over his hair.

He grabs the packet of paint swatches, the colors we'd chosen marked with an "x." "Ready?" he asks.

The bundle of cash from our wedding is warm in my wallet. After the darkness of the city streets, the florescent lights and high ceilings of the nearly empty store make me dizzy. We lay our paint samples on the counter and order our colors, hypnotized by the large mixers. When the machines are done, the salesperson opens each lid, dabs the cover with a single dot of paint. "Great colors," he says. "They'll go well together."

I wonder what we look like: young couple at Home Depot near closing time on a weeknight, buying six gallons of color. Our sweatshirts and jackets, our crossed arms and caps. I wonder if the exhaustion shows on our faces—the fact that we've waited two and a half months to buy this paint. That we've spent evenings dreaming up colors, imagining possible browns and greens. Our cart lists under the weight of it all. We pay with cash and push the cart into the parking lot, where we load our six gallons into the trunk.

When we return home, I go straight to bed, but Kevin starts taping the kitchen. "I'm going to start tomorrow," he says as he squats near the trim, tape in hand, the two greens we'd purchased like sentinels in the corner.

That fall, Binghamton turns gray and rainy. The yellow and red trees that made me thankful each time the bus crossed the river to campus are now bare, their branches gray like they will be all winter. The dryer in the basement of our apartment breaks and it takes nearly a month for the landlords to replace it. We spend late October and November drying clothing on the outdoor clothesline and, more often, on a drying rack in the kitchen. Damp sweaters and jeans perpetually transform the biggest room in the apartment into a series of passageways. Our towels are stiff. Our jeans and shirts oddly unwrinkled in some parts, warped from the drying rack's bars in others. I read books and grade papers in the living room, wrapped in blankets. Kevin works the closing shift and doesn't return until midnight. I grow bored quickly, standing up to make tea every forty-five minutes. The floors creak as I pace with my mug; everyone seems so far away.

We paint the kitchen in shifts. Kevin puts on the first coat while I'm on campus. I return that evening to locked doors and an empty apartment but to a kitchen with a sudden blush of "dill weed."

After the kitchen we begin the dining room, largely because it has the least amount of furniture to move. We spread the plastic sheeting over the wood floors, tape the ceiling and floor, pour the blue paint into the tray. I do the trim, Kevin takes the roller, and together we turn the white walls a smoky blue.

"This is great," Kevin says. The blue paint frames the white trim of the doorway to the kitchen, where the two hues of green glow in the afternoon light. I get paint on my arms, paint on my elbows, even a bit of blue paint in my hair. "What am I going to do with you?" Kevin asks, and we are laughing.

Just as we finish the first coat, Kevin's phone rings. "Put me on speakerphone," his mom chokes, her voice tight so that everything she says comes out in a burst of breath. "It's Grandpa," she says. "He hasn't been feeling well. We just got back the test results." She takes a deep breath, swallows, tries to start but then must swallow again.

Kevin frowns, the press of his eyebrows deepening his eye sockets. He doesn't look at me but at the floor and then the roller in his hand, which drips onto the plastic.

"It's liver cancer," his mother finally manages. "They're only giving him three months."

"Three months?" Kevin asks, monotone, unlike a question.

"That's what they say. Anyway," his mom says, starting to cry again, "I thought you should know. Pray for him, okay? And take care of each other."

When Kevin hangs up, he says he's going to wash off his roller.

"You okay?" I ask.

"Yes. I just need to wash this. I need to get ready for work."

He carries it through the kitchen, letting the screen door bang as he passes through.

I put the lid back over the can of paint and drape plastic wrap over the paint tray so it doesn't dry out before I put on the second coat. The door bangs again as Kevin enters the kitchen, but he goes directly to the office, where he prints out a photograph. "I think we should send this to Grandpa with the thank you note from the wedding," he says. "And probably soon."

In the photograph, Kevin kneels in his brown tuxedo next to his grandfather, who sits in a wheelchair and rests his head against three fingers. His eyes are milky behind his glasses, his boutonniere tilted. He half smiles, one corner of his mouth lifted, but not enough to show any teeth. He had been in the hospital three days before the wedding. When Kevin had called him, he told Kevin that he would break out of the hospital for the wedding, no matter what the doctors said.

"Your grandpa would like getting that picture," I say.

Kevin nods. "Yes, he would. He really wanted to make it to the wedding. He made sure of it."

"I'm glad he did."

Kevin nods again. "Me too."

That evening, while Kevin works, I put the second coat on in the dining room. I pull in lamps from the office and living room to help me see. I make long, smooth strokes with the roller and watch the way the paint darkens as it dries. When I finish, I carry the brushes and rollers to the basement sink. I hold my hands under the water, massage the brushes and rollers to help get off the paint.

The water turns a heavy blue. We aren't sure we'll get back to the Midwest for the holidays. Flights are so expensive, especially with Kevin only working part-time. I begin to shiver. We shouldn't be here, I think. It was wrong to move so far away. The selfishness of our decision sticks to the bristles. I hunch over the sink, using my fingernails to strip paint from the brush, but it takes a long time for the water to clear.

Even with two rooms painted, the apartment, as well as the city, still seems so strange: the white walls, the neighborhood sidewalks we explore on evening walks, the width of our queen bed. We argue most about money and chores: if we have enough to travel home for Christmas and visit Kevin's grandfather; whether to let the dishes soak or to wash them with a cloth as the sink fills with water. Some evenings I ache from the effort of it all, and I begin to wonder what my mother and grandmothers experienced when they were first married, when they first moved to new homes. I want to ask them how they *felt*—what they thought when they sat alone in the dark, waiting for husbands to come home, for the rooms to feel familiar, for this distribution of chores and tasks to ease its way into routine.

But when I call my mom on weekends, I find such questions impossible to ask. My questions have a hardness, a grittiness I can't capture in words, and so I tell her we are doing well—we are painting the apartment, one room at a time, that we work in shifts and sometimes hardly see each other. "Yes," I say. "Yesterday I got home from work, and the doors were all locked, the car gone, but the living room had been taped. Kevin even pushed the futon into the middle and left the paint tray on the plastic tarp."

My mother laughs, and I laugh, and we say goodbye, but when I hang up, my ear buzzes with silence.

I warm up yesterday's lentil soup for dinner. I eat alone in the dining room, my feet hooked around the legs of the chair. Afterward, I change into an old T-shirt and turn on the radio loud enough that it fills the corners of the room. I open the paint can with a screwdriver, stir the thick, yellowish brown paint. "Campground," the label had said. It is the color I'm most worried about—something bordering on ugly, like the canvas of old tents. But Kevin had liked it—had said it reminded him of our camping trips on the Mississippi River and the North Shore.

Moving here took faith for both of us. When we loaded the moving van, we trusted that the program I was entering would advance my career, that Kevin would find a job that was both meaningful and rewarding. When I first told him I wanted to apply to another graduate program even though we'd already been living apart for two years, he said he would go wherever I ended up. His flexibility had felt like a gift. But now that he's still just a barista, I worry he'll begin to resent me. I've dragged him across the country, not unlike the way my father and grandfather have propelled their own families' moves. We lack a community here, and with his own grandfather so ill, how could Kevin not long to be back in Wisconsin?

In the books I've been reading, Wendell Berry and Scott Russell Sanders both sometimes equate a commitment to place with a marriage. We must "marry ourselves to a place," Sanders writes, in order to fully "commune with other creatures" and "make ourselves at home through stories." Berry even argues, "No matter how much one may love the world as a whole, one can live fully in it only by living responsibly in some small part of it." As if fidelity somehow strengthens our connection to the earth in the same way it can strengthen a connection with a lover: offering a deeper, more spiritually sustaining experience of life.

I want to believe them, to believe that the commitment I've made to Kevin will be a good one and that the same kind of commitment could enrich my experience of place.

I'd like to think when I am old, my joints stiff, my bony fingers gripping a mug of tea, that I will look out my window and see something I have been a part of, something I have contributed to. Something that has defined me just as much as I have defined it. I will see trees and sky, a now-fallow garden. I will see organizations and communities that I have been a part of and that will continue on after I am gone. I don't want to look out my window at a location I have only lived at for a few years, a few months, maybe—a location like this one, viewed out of these half-painted walls, and not see my own history interlaced with its climate, its weather, its flora and fauna. To realize I've moved through life, looking at what is best for me rather than considering what I can give to the diverse, complex communities of which I am a part.

And yet here I am—here we are—in a new place, where we know no one. Where we don't intend to stay long.

What have we done? I wonder as I pour the paint into the tray and prepare the roller. *What have we done?* The paint goes on thick. The walls drink it in so that I have to refill the tray more quickly than we did in the other rooms. As I wipe paint drips on my jeans and lift the roller to the wall, the fears keep coming, cyclical, insistent: that I am not committing to place, though I need to. That I'm holding myself apart from the world around me. That Kevin and I, in moving and distancing ourselves from our communities, are sabotaging our marriage as well. I maneuver behind the bookshelf and the television. I lug a dining room chair from corner to corner so that I can reach the top of the walls. My arms grow tired, my hands numb. But I continue. I clench my jaw and imagine Kevin returning to a room bright with light.

For more than a week, we spend our days circling each other with paintbrushes, tracing each other's presences by washrags on the clothesline and lighter cans of paint. We finish the living room, then the bedroom, then the bathroom, until finally only the office remains. Kevin gets a day off on a Tuesday, and even though I have a stack of papers to grade and a book to read, we decide to paint the office. It will be the first, and only room, that we start and finish together.

We've saved this room for last because of the bookcases. They nearly touch the ceiling and are so crammed with books that the shelves sag in the middle. The thought of moving those bookcases in order to paint the walls behind them does not excite me. But it is the last room, and we are together, and the sun has come out after a week of cool rain. Bread dough rises on the counter, filling the air with the heady scent of yeast. From the office's two door-ways, the blues of the dining room and bedroom give way to the greens of the kitchen and the burnt umber of the bathroom. We ease the bookcases forward a few inches at a time, cringing when they scrape at the wood floor.

"I can't wait to have this done," Kevin says, laying down the plastic.

I stir the paint and pour it into the trays. A light brown this time, chosen to match the brown on the map of Sawbill and Brule that we'd hung above the desk in August. It's the brown of bare ground near a fire pit, or the shady area where tree roots merge into soil.

We turn on the radio and work in silence, only speaking when one of us needs to refill a tray. I put the bread in the oven, return to the office, take the bread out. Soon enough, the walls sparkle from wet paint—the project complete.

"Do you like it?" I ask, my voice high pitched with hope.

"Yes. Do you?"

"Yes, I do," I say, but my throat tightens. I need him to more than like it; I need this to prove worthwhile. The trays and rollers and bookcases lay like a minefield between us—the room growing larger, Kevin too far away to touch. I pick dried paint from my fingernails. "Does it feel like home?"

Kevin pauses. "No," he says.

I swallow—fight off a sting in my eyes. He is right. Nothing I do can make this process easy. I imagine the winter ahead of us: the snow on the ground and the air like ice between here and the Midwest.

Kevin continues. "But maybe it's starting to."

I nod. While Kevin takes the paint supplies to the basement, I rehang the map of the Boundary Waters. The browns match perfectly, so that the map's frame and the blue of the lakes seem to emerge out of the wall.

"It's perfect," I say. "A good color."

I heat water on the stove and cut two slices of bread. It is late, and I am tired, but I refuse to go to bed. I carry the bread and two mugs of tea to the living room, where I wait for the walls to sustain us.

THE DECKLED EDGE

❧ KEVIN'S GRANDFATHER PASSES away three months after we finish painting the apartment. We book a last-minute flight to Milwaukee, landing just as the state's largest blizzard in more than fifty years closes the airport. In the final moments of the airplane's landing, as the plane tilts to the left and right so that I grip the armrests and worry one wing and then the other will scrape against the ground, I think: *this is what it's like to be on a downed plane.* But the plane lands safely, snow obscuring anything past the ends of the wings, and Kevin's mother waits at the nearly empty pick-up lane.

"I'm so glad you've made it. My children are here," Kevin's mother says, giving us each a quick hug as we throw our luggage into the back of her Scion and get into the car. The wipers flip back and forth with a shrill squeak. Up ahead, beyond the overhang, snow whitens the road and sky so that all we can see is the gray mass of it, vague and unending, not unlike how I feel, back in Milwaukee for the first time after the wedding and the holidays, unsure how to act. My face is not long with grief, like Kevin's and his mother's. Only tired from travel—from the endless hours at the Detroit airport, where we drank coffee and waited through flight delay after flight delay. "Maybe they'll postpone the funeral if we don't make it," Kevin said, his foot bouncing on the floor like it always does when he's nervous. "Don't worry, we'll get there," I replied, though I wasn't entirely sure myself. If I were suspended upside down from the ceiling, twirling in an odd-colored light, I would have said the same thing about the flight, about the funeral, about marriage: *Don't worry, we'll get there. It will be all right.*

When we wake up the next morning, a five-foot snowdrift blocks the front door of my mother-in-law's apartment. I make coffee, eat a bowl of cereal, and then help shovel a path through the snowdrift so that my mother-in-law's thirteen-year-old lapdog can get outside. At first, I don't bother with a shovel. The snowdrift—like those captured in my grandma's winter photographs of Sawbill— is too high and compact for a simple shovel. Instead, I plow through with my body, using my hands to push at the snow on each side of me, to propel myself forward. The snow gets beneath my scarf, piercing my neck, but I feel more alert than I have all morning. I smile and laugh and shiver, kicking at the snow with my feet, while Kevin neatens my "path" with his shovel and his mother laughs from the front door. Afterward, we drink more coffee and sort through his grandfather's military metals, pinning them to a board for the wake. Boxes of photographs and metals and paperwork fill the living room. Kevin's mother sighs and says she's going to shower.

I begin to flip through the boxes of photographs. It is the only task I can think to do as my mother-in-law cries in the bathroom, my sister-in-law re-hems a dress, and Kevin digs out something from somewhere in the garage. I tell myself it will help me learn more about his family and connect with their grief, but really it's to look at his grandmother. I have never met Kevin's grandmother. Not this one, at least. But as I look through the photographs, I am drawn to her just the same—her high forehead, her slightly squashed nose, her constant smile. In each and every photograph spread across my mother-in-law's living room floor, the grandmother could be twelve, sixteen. She never seems to get older: eighteen-year-old Phyllis in the fake fur coat. Twenty-year-old Phyllis with the child (Kevin's mom?) on her hip. It doesn't matter what location, what age. Always the tall, slender figure, the quiet sense of joy.

Here, I think, as I sort through the photographs—*here is a woman who lived*. Here is a woman who, at age twenty, wrapped an arm around a friend's shoulder, ran through the streets of her small town in high heels, rushed home from work at the factory to see if she'd received a letter from Russ. What did she think when the telegraph came—Russ asking for $50—*will explain later?* What would she think if she knew her family would laugh at that telegraph as they unearthed it during a February blizzard? What would she think of the Russ, who at ninety, had died in a hospital bed, his nose wider than it was in those early photographs of the two of them on a bench by the park, he in his brown military uniform (pressed now and hanging on the door for the wake), she in that thin, blue dress?

"Mom was a saint," my mother-in-law says later when I show her the photographs. "Such a saint." My mother-in-law presses her hand on my shoulder. I stiffen, fight the urge to shrug it off, and then wonder if she can feel me stiffen. My mother-in-law, who is not my mother but whose father has just died. My mother-in-law who'd hugged me when I'd arrived with Kevin. Had said, "My children are home." My mother-in-law who makes Kevin and I sleep in her bed—the only double in the apartment. And so we sleep in her bed, the photograph of the grandmother with the high forehead and youthful face on the nightstand, staring at me with her youth and her joy, staring while I lay awake, until I can't help but fall in love with the face. A face that says, *I know what it's like to be in a strange house, a strange bed. Decades ago, you could have been me.*

At the wake, a line of veterans overflow the funeral home's foyer, old men that slump slightly even as they straighten their caps, adjust their belts, and wait for the service. I walk around the main room, stare at the pictures I'd sorted, now tacked to foam poster board or projected onto a screen—Russ and Phyllis on the park bench. Russ and Phyllis in front of the church.

I take another mint from the bowl on the end table and wonder if the funeral director is watching me. If he is—and if he has counted all twelve mints I've eaten—he must know I don't belong. He must think I'm here for the refreshments and performance.

I skirt conversations, gatherings of people who haven't seen each other since Phyllis's funeral, eighteen years ago. I can't find Kevin. His grief for his grandfather, who'd been more like a father, has turned to nervous energy, forcing him to stay busy, to keep from looking at the coffin, at the thick nose, the too-short hair, the crooked lips. I had followed him earlier as he moved from one group of people to another, but after a while I'd begun to feel like a small child, always tagging behind, and so I had paused and let him wander. Yet standing here by the poster board, sucking on my thirteenth mint, I still feel silly. My stomach begins to cramp. I haven't brought enough black clothes. I rub at the salt stains on my shoes, the coffee stain on my shirt. I should have washed them, but we hadn't had time after the phone call, when we suddenly had to pack our bags and book a flight before all the airports closed from the blizzard.

Kevin's mother approaches me. "Diane, this is Jennie, Kevin's wife," she says, and I shake the hand of a stranger, a woman with cropped gray hair, a pearl necklace, and an abundance of citrus perfume.

"Ah, the newlyweds!" the woman replies. "So nice to meet you. Sorry I couldn't make it to the wedding."

"That's okay." I smile. I open my mouth to say something else—though I'm not sure what—but my mother-in-law and the citrus-smelling woman have already moved on to a man in a corduroy suit.

I'm still not used to it: "The newlyweds." The label feels like gauze draped over my head, the ends tucked under my shoes. So strange to be a "wife" next to people who've worn the word for decades—had to get their rings resized not just once but three times—after the babies, when the fingers swelled, and then after the bout with pneumonia. All those anniversary earrings and necklaces, the long silences, one person moving past the other in the hallway, the shoulders touching. The recliners reforming themselves to widening girths.

I twist the ring on my finger. I take another mint.

One month after the wedding Kevin and I had argued for the first time. Not a little argument about how to best wash the dishes or sort the clothes, but a large argument—something about spending habits and debt and whether or not we were already sabotaging the lives we wanted for ourselves—an argument that left us tense and angry so that for three days our silences grated against the walls and left so much dust on the floor that we walked softly and slowly through the hallways. For three evenings I enclosed myself in the bedroom and thought fully, for the first time, about what it meant to be stuck to this man forever. Any extrication would be slow and painful. We'd never erase each other from our lives.

As I'd lain in bed after that argument, the corners of the room had darkened. Kevin's side of the bed grew away from me, flat and cold. My throat tightened. We should have bought lighter furniture, I thought—not the armoire and dresser, finished with such dark stain. How heavy everything looked, I thought. How heavy.

During the memorial service, a similar heaviness falls over the room. I sit next to Kevin's mother and sister and pretend to look how I think I should look—somber, my lips pressed together, my eyebrows thoughtful, perplexed. When the two National Guards-men—women with stiff torsos and spotless white gloves, all too young—unfold and refold the flag, handing it to Kevin's uncle, I place my hand on Kevin's knee and feel him lean into me. When the car alarm goes off just as Kevin and the other pallbearers slide the coffin into the back of the hearse, I laugh with everyone, their stifled sobs bubbling into two or three chortles then calming into a shake of the head, an ease of the shoulders. The funeral goes well and so does the luncheon after, and we return to the apartment to eat cold pasta salad for dinner while watching the news.

Only then do the walls crowd in on me—the small two-bedroom apartment, the items stacked and scattered across the living room floor, the dishes piled in the sink and the poster board covering the kitchen table. I do not want to be here. I'm sick of Kevin's family, of people I do not know. Sick of standing awkwardly in a corner, of trying so hard to appear sympathetic. I need to get out and away from it all. I need to relax the muscles in my face.

"Want to go for a walk?" I ask Kevin, but he shakes his head no, and so I sit there, my jaw clenched, until we all go to bed.

That night, I slip from beneath the covers, stand, and walk to the doorway. Kevin snores on his side, his legs bent and pulled toward his stomach, his mouth slack. My mother-in-law snores from the other room, where she sleeps in the twin bed Kevin used while in high school. The dog pokes his nose from the doorway.

I wrap a blanket around my shoulders and make my way into the living room, to the box full of pictures, to the young wife.

1939, the beach by the lighthouse. A group of girls, thin arms and legs, point their toes for the picture. Their suits sag at the hips from moisture. Their hair plasters itself to bronzed foreheads.

They are oblivious to the strangeness of it all: those confident girls before the war, knowing nothing about the future, nothing about age and the ways their bodies would change, the ways their swimsuits would go out of style, so that now, when I look at them, I can hardly believe girls like that, girls then, would jut a shoulder forward, heave their chests as if sure of their beauty, their specialness. They do not realize how ordinary they are. They will work in factories and then raise children. They will die in the towns of their birth.

I run my fingers along the photograph's deckled edges and flip to the back, but the back is blank. Was this before they were married? After? I cannot tell the grandmother's age—Phyllis in her twenties is hardly different from Phyllis in her thirties, only distinguishable, really, from Phyllis in her seventies, the Phyllis who died after surgery, who spent two months in a coma in the living room, seventy-year-old Russ with the large nose and the brown recliner bending over her each day, turning her from side to side, rubbing her feet while the hospice nurse changed her IV.

In the darkness of my mother-in-law's living room at 2:00 a.m., I realize, with embarrassment, that I am crying. I hold my breath, press the corners of my eyes. What if my mother-in-law comes out? Or Kevin's sister? I wish I were home—not the home Kevin and I have made, with the dark, antique furniture we'd purchased with wedding money one Sunday afternoon—but "home" home, with my parents, in the bedroom no longer mine. I wish I were with my mother. My mother would hug me. She would pretend I was still young. "You look so grown up," my mother had said at the rehearsal dinner, to me in my black high heels, the floral cocktail dress, the white cardigan. And then later that evening: "That's more like it. That's my girl," this time to me in the worn jeans, the green sweatshirt, the loose strands of hair and the slightly smelly shoes that Kevin wanted me to throw out.

The following night, after Kevin had unbuttoned all the buttons of my dress and I'd changed into the black lingerie my sister had given me as a bachelorette gift, my parents had called: "Want to join us in the lounge for wine and cake?" they asked. And the next morning, another call: "Want to join us for coffee?"

I had smiled, had almost laughed, and then bit my lip—knowing I wanted to say yes, to be with my parents a bit longer, to not make that split.

Was it like that for my own mother? For my grandmothers? For Kevin's grandmother? As Phyllis stood next to Russ in front of that church, wearing that white dress, fitting her arm around his arm, around the brown jacket, as she clung to his hand, knowing he'd ship out soon, did she look back at her parents—those silent figures in darker, thicker photographs, wearing coarse fabric and a wilting corsage—and feel something like loss?

Yes, I think. Yes. She must have. She must have. The thought comforts me—everything has been done before. Couples have begun lives together. They have fought and died together. They have left families and formed new ones, have made new homes. Twenty, forty, sixty years ago, they, too, felt the sudden tangibility of tradition—the gauze tucked under their shoes, the wedding band on the counter throwing its small shadow.

The dog noses his way into the living room. The refrigerator shudders and makes its small hum. From the photograph, the grandmother smiles—that high forehead, that quiet sense of joy— smiles at the laundry on the clothesline, the blue sky, the flowers in front of the church—smiles at the telegraph and the drip of the IV—smiles at me, legs crossed in my mother-in-law's recliner, the chipped remains of nail polish still on my toes from the wedding four months before. *You could have been me. You could have been me*, she whispers, and though I do not know this woman—have never met her—I want to believe her.

PIECING

❧ WHEN I AM nineteen—well before I become infatuated with Sawbill but late enough in my adolescence that I have already begun to see in my grandmother a pattern for myself—I fly alone for the first time to visit her in Utah. I leave Minneapolis in the morning, have an hour-and-a-half layover in Phoenix, and then catch the Las Vegas/St. George airport shuttle for the final two-hour leg of my journey. At the shuttle's last stop, my grandpa leans against a wall, his hands in the back of sagging jeans, and my grandma stands on her tiptoes, trying to peer into the shuttle's dark windows. Only when I emerge does she relax, elbowing forward to give me a bony hug.

"I hope the flight wasn't too long," she says after my grandpa has picked up my suitcase and is driving us to their one-level townhouse with its red-tiled roof. "Is there anything special you wanted to do this week?"

I shrug. From the age of twelve, when I'd learned to quilt, my grandma and I had spent a week together each summer in Minnesota completing a project. But ever since they moved to southwest Utah two years ago, I haven't been able to bring my sewing machine along. Plus, this time we only have four days.

I follow my grandma into the guest bedroom, where I set my bag down. The quilts in the rack mark the passing of time: the pieced tulip wall hanging she'd made five summers ago, when they still lived at the lake home, draped next to the pinwheel baby quilt completed just before they moved. "Would you like to see what I've been working on?" she asks, a hand on the closet doorknob. The hinges creak, emitting the soft scent of rosewater, and as she reaches for a stack of fabric on the top shelf, a large bag falls to the ground with a thump. Inside: a twin-sized Grandmother's Flower Garden, made from six rows of hexagonal flowers, all posed on a yellow background.

"What's this?" I ask. I remember starting my own a few years before, cutting enough fabric and paper templates for seven flowers before finding the hand piecing too tedious.

She glances at it; "Oh, that old thing. I don't know why I keep it. I'll never finish it." She lays it out on the guest bed, and we both begin to run our fingers across the seams. Definitely a work of the seventies—fuchsia and purple next to an aquamarine plaid, a ketchup-red print beside green ferns and blue flowers.

"Mmm. I like it," I say. And I do. I have grown a fondness for ugly things—for ugly, overlooked fabric that, when sewn into a quilt, becomes necessary to a larger pattern. The larger pattern, in fact, more arresting in its beauty because of the ugliness of its scraps.

I picture the quilt in my quilt rack or spread across my bed. It demands attention.

My grandma picks at a red thread stuck on one of the flowers and tries to smooth the wrinkles with her hand. "Really?" she asks; "Well then, you should take it home with you. I was just going to throw it away." And without another comment she rolls the quilt up and places it in a plastic bag.

All week long, as my grandparents show me around their new

home, I peek into my suitcase and poke at the unfinished edges—the basted, unquilted layers somehow raw. My grandma has often given me quilting items—I owe much of my fabric to her, as well as my sewing machine—but this quilt, incomplete and disregarded, speaks to me of a sadness my grandma cannot articulate—a loneliness I cannot ignore.

Back in Minnesota, I put the bag in my closet, intending to work on it later in the summer. But soon I am packing clothes again to return to college, the quilt pushed aside in the last-minute rush for bedding and almost-forgotten sweaters.

A photograph: my grandma and I on the La Crosse Queen, a steam-driven paddleboat, during the last of my summer visits to her home in Dakota, Minnesota. My grandma, short and sturdy without looking overweight, lets her arms hang at her sides, and in the shadow her hands appear clenched. Large sunglasses block her eyes. Her lips curve into a slight smile. The thin black strap of her purse pulls at the collar of her blouse, and her hair almost matches the white of the railing—the white of the life preserver.

I stand next to her, slightly taller and somehow underdressed in shorts and a striped pastel T-shirt. That summer I had cut my hair shorter than I ever had before—no strand more than two inches long. In the photograph, I have pulled my bangs away from my face with a bobby pin and finger a purse I had made of the fabric squares my grandma gave me the year before.

I make a watercolor painting of the photograph in my art class that fall. In the painting, my grandma sits on the plastic deck chair in the upper level, gazing across the Mississippi River at the shore. The blue awning darkens her face and so she looks blue too, her white hair tinted with a cerulean dye.

I paint the picture because of her stillness, because it captures what I then think of as her essence—her hands in her lap, her face turned as if sad. She frowns slightly in the summer sun. She will soon move to Utah, though I know she doesn't want to, though I know she hates the heat. When she moves, she will place her quilts in boxes and tape them shut, and who knows when or where she will open them? It is my pity and my frustration that I mix into that blue wash and spread over the shadows of her shirt.

My art teacher hangs the painting in the display case for three weeks.

When my grandma sees the finished watercolor, she says she looks fat. She doesn't realize all that it means to me, of the summers it memorializes: our fingers touching fabric and ripping seams, our tongues licking the fraying tips of thread; summers when she'd serve tea in white mugs that we'd hold with lifted pinkies; when we'd take evening drives on Highway 90, the road dipping down and sweeping along bluffs so rounded and massive I had to crane my neck to see their tops. Those summers, before my grandpa decided his arthritis could no longer tolerate Minnesota winters, were "stack and slash" quilt classes at the local historical society, blue and green dresses flapping on country clotheslines, and the hiss of the iron on starched cotton. They were miniature quiche on small cream plates and my grandma laughing with her quilting friends. They were quilt shows and trips to the fabric store, bolts of every color in a line like paint strokes. In my journals from those years, I wrote of tradition and beauty. I said I was content, my grandma standing behind me, patting my shoulder while I worked with her sewing machine. As if I fulfilled something for her. As if, with her, I returned to some other world.

And at that time, during those earlier summers, I suppose I did. But it is the passing of that world that I memorialize in the painting—a passing emphasized by the fact that my grandma cannot see it. She has moved to Utah, and I will soon start college in a small river town just north of her old home in Dakota, Minnesota.

In preparation, I pack three quilts along with my miniature refrigerator, my bundle of clothing, and my shower caddy. When my grandma asks if I'm going to bring the sewing machine, I say no, not at first. I tell her I'm not sure how busy I will be—if I will have time. She understands and agrees.

Yet by this point, I am lying. I am not worried about being busy. I am worried about being seen. I want my new roommate to think of me as a hiker, not a quilter. There is a difference, I understand, between owning a quilt and making a quilt. I do not want to be the girl with mousy hair who slouches in front of the sewing machine, squinting as she guides two triangles beneath the foot, her nose warmed by the machine's small light bulb. The girl who sits in her chair and sews while others straighten their hair in the bathroom before strapping rollerblades to their feet. No, I leave the sewing machine at home to accumulate dust. And when I do bring a project to school—a queen-sized Prairie Queen quilt that needs its binding hand-stitched to the backing, or the Grandmother's Flower Garden quilt later on, I hide it in a box in the closet and only unearth it when my roommates are gone and the door locked.

My grandma begins the Grandmother's Flower Garden quilt, with its tiny, toothed stitches, shortly after my grandparents leave Sawbill. My grandpa relocated to London a year before for his job with Honeywell, and in 1981 she follows him. She lives in a house called Church Cottage in Old Windsor and goes to jumble sales to stay busy. She refuses to drive in England because she fears the turnpikes, and she cannot work because she doesn't have the proper visa. At the jumble sales, she searches for old clothing that she thinks might make a good quilt. A woman's indigo housedress, with small pink flowers. A man's plaid shirt. A brown paisley apron. Back at the house she and Grandpa rent, she washes the clothing and cuts it into 825 three-inch hexagons. She then begins to hand-piece them into rings that resemble flowers.

All through college, I think of the quilt—of my grandma assembling a scrap quilt out of other people's clothing, out of clothing she purchased at British rummage sales. And I think of the fact that I can complete the quilt, can finish the tasks she has left undone and pick up the needle forgotten on the armrest. I only need to decide.

Another photograph: my grandma at her home in Dakota, Minnesota, leaning forward in a chair, her elbows resting on her knees. Her eyes meet the lens of the camera, but she does not smile—as if I have caught her contemplating a burden and she has not yet had a chance to paste on a different expression. The ceiling-to-floor curtains behind her are stiff with a leaden weight, with leaden folds. On the wooden stand next to the chair sits a basket of artificial flowers.

After I take the picture she asks why—why do I want the picture of her? I say because of the light. The way the light through the window has turned her hair into a halo.

Across the room, the camera warm in my hands, I relax into the textured cloth of the chair.

"Have you been quilting much?" my grandma asks, and I describe the Bow Tie quilt. I have just finished the top, and she is anxious to see it. When she smiles, I notice how thin her lips are. Not thick like mine.

"How about you, Grandma?" I ask. "How are your projects going?"

She sighs and looks toward the window, where a neighbor cuts grass. "Oh, I haven't done much lately. Grandpa and I've been too busy packing." She dreads the upcoming move to Utah—the condensing of possessions until everything can fit into a two-bedroom townhouse. She leans back in her chair and the skin on her cheek-bones sags. In the recently vacuumed carpet, our footprints lead to the chairs. "Would you like some fabric?" she asks. "I can't bring it all. There's not enough room . . ."

Her eyes water, her lips purse, and her face reddens in spots, like they always do at the end of family visits, when she tells us not to make the beds or do the dishes—she needs something to keep her occupied.

She is only giving me the fabric, I know, because she is moving, and she does not want to move.

"Sure," I quickly, self-consciously reply. "I'll take any fabric you don't want."

I imagine the bins that smell like the air freshener she keeps in the bathroom, the prints they contain, ironed and folded and sorted by color, labeled with the names of the quilt patterns she had intended to use. Enough for four quilts. Perhaps five or six. I long to lay the fabric on the floor—to touch each one.

I imagine her face when she waves goodbye from the driveway. The way we always pretend not to notice her tears.

I imagine the emptiness of her closets in St. George.

"Sure, I'll take any fabric you don't want." The words leave a grit in my mouth.

For years, when I am in college, I blame my grandpa for forcing my grandma to move, and although I eventually realize that the situation was likely more complicated than that—marriages require compromises no teenager can understand—it affects the way I view quilting. During those summers in Dakota, Grandpa had always been a shadowy figure. He often attended archery tournaments with other retired seniors during the day, and he went to bed early. I spoke to him only during dinner, when my grandma and I would move our quilting projects off of the dining room table so that we could sit and eat. Grandma always started cooking around 4:30, and I often offered to help. One day she asked me to cook the bacon for BLTs. I had never cooked real bacon before, only imitation turkey, and I winced as the grease sizzled and spit, landing on my arm. Once the translucent fat had solidified, I carried the plate of bacon to the table where my grandpa already sat, staring outside at the weathered fence and the wooded ravine behind it.

"Look Grandpa," my grandma said, "Jennie made the bacon all by herself!" She squeezed my shoulder, and I distinctly recall the boniness of her fingers and the pride in her eyes. I had made bacon. Her granddaughter could quilt and make bacon.

My grandpa looked up from his seat and said something appropriate for the trivial accomplishment thrust into his gaze. I held my tongue between my teeth and pretended to smile, though it disturbed me—the entire situation: my summer suddenly tainted by a tightening fear that I was being domesticated, forced to fulfill a function I could only associate with the swipe of a damp rag on dishes and the echo of men in the living room.

All summer I wanted to ask her why she was moving—why she agreed to go. Couldn't she stay in Minnesota and let Grandpa go by himself? Couldn't they become snowbirds, and at least return for long summers? But I could not ask those questions, just as, today, I cannot admit how much I wish she'd never left.

My grandma's father died when she was young, forcing my grandma's mother to provide a stable income. When I ask my grandma about her childhood, she says, "I wish now that my mother had taught me more about hand quilting, but she worked all the time and just didn't get around to it."

In her relationship with me, perhaps my grandma sees herself fulfilling what her own grandmother wasn't able to do—her own grandmother who died when my grandma was six, unable to teach her how to quilt, unable to pass on the Grandmother's Flower Garden blocks that she had not yet finished. When my grandma gives me fabric, she attempts to salvage a connection that should never have broken. When she thinks of those Grandmother's Flower Garden blocks her own grandmother once started, she only sighs. Her sister has them—has kept them, though they are not yet complete.

My grandparents drop off the bins of fabric the spring before they move to St. George.

"Well, should we get them?" my grandpa asks in our foyer, his face square and tan, dotted with liver spots. Shadows flit against the pale walls.

My grandma looks at him. She holds his gaze. "I suppose."

I am sixteen, a junior in high school. I slip on my shoes to help unload the truck and suddenly doubt myself. For, as we empty the bed of its three blue tubs, my grandma refuses to look at me. Perhaps it is hesitation. Perhaps regret. But when my eyes meet hers, she glances away, and she does not smile.

The image unsettles me. At college, I do not tell anyone that I quilt, but I often spend afternoons in the library, reading about the women of the 1970s who, bolstered by the bicentennial and the rebirth of the women's liberation movement, revived the craft. Some had never sewn before and signed up for community quilting classes. Others learned from their mothers and grandmothers. The resurgence excited so many that the textile industry, for the first time since the invention of polyester, again began to produce large quantities of cotton fabric. It was a time to claim pride in one's heritage. To participate in and celebrate a craft that had almost died out. Some women preferred the traditional patterns of their grandmothers. Others, especially artists who saw quilting as a means of feminist expression, sought to create a new art form.

By combining jarring colors and painstaking appliqué, they crafted wall hangings fit for contemporary art galleries. For them, quilting became a political act, a statement of identity.

But what, I wonder from my small table in the library, did it mean for the others?

My grandma, then a mother of four, signed up for her first quilting class in the 1970s. Twenty years later, she taught me to quilt. I have gone to quilt guild meetings with her, and I have attended quilt shows with her, but still I cannot answer that question for myself. What does quilting mean to me? Or, rather, what does it mean for me to quilt? I struggle when comparing my image of myself as a quilter with the image that I perceive to be associated with quilting. The question then becomes, what does it mean to quilt when 95 percent of the hobby's participants are still female?

In my journals that year I tell myself that "eventually I will come to accept my place as a modern quilter. Eventually, I will learn to share my interest in quilting with pride." But even as I write them, such statements clang, metallic and hollow.

The summer of 2005, my grandparents drive me along rural Utah highways, where red dirt and crushed rock forms a dust I cannot scrub from my feet. I suck on a mint, fighting carsickness, and feel invisible.

I can't imagine living here, in this land abandoned by two continental plates, and I wonder why my grandparents have moved so often. None of my dad's siblings were born in the same place, and each move continues to take my grandparents farther away from their living relatives—their living friends. *Why Utah?* I ask myself. All the plants die such dry and brittle deaths. I swear that I will never live in a place with so little green.

When my grandpa had a heart attack in the spring, my grandma waited in the hospital thirty-two hours before calling any relatives. Now she listens for his movements while we drink iced tea on the patio. The oleanders I helped her plant bloom their pink, orange, and white petals. I ask her if she misses Dakota. "If Grandpa died, I would return to Minnesota in a heartbeat," she says. She circles the rim of her glass with her finger, eyes focused somewhere beyond the brown haze of the horizon, before asking if I need more tea.

That evening, we walk to the swimming pool. My grandma sits in a chair in the shade with a book, a sun visor, and a bottle of water. I unzip my shorts and wish I had brought my other bathing suit, the one-piece I wear for gym, instead of this—a tankini with a rather pronounced V-neck. Beads of sweat evaporate with a glitter from the crease near my elbow. My arms swing, toned and solid, while my grandma's pale flesh lays over the plastic armrest like a blanket. I tread water for fifteen minutes and then do the back-stroke. My grandma looks up every once in a while to fan herself with the book, her smile bleached and translucent. I wonder if I make her feel old, if she comprehends the world I've grown up in, with its cell phones and Starbucks coffee shops and colleges offering eighty different majors. I spread out my arms and float, letting the ripples from my backstroke lap at my skin, a cool tickle where water meets air.

When I imagine my grandma in England, hand stitching the Flower Garden quilt, I envision her with firm arms and hair still naturally blonde. Alone in the rented house, she grows weary of the rain and buses, the dirty lace window treatments that even bleach doesn't clean. She calls my father, a student at the University of Minnesota, but he doesn't pick up. She waits long evenings for my grandpa to come home. Rain blots the windows so that all she can see is her frizzy hair and the circles under her eyes.

Restless, she walks to rummage sales, where she meanders through aisles, touching porcelain figurines, Queen Victoria thimbles, and stained tea towels. Before long, her fingers grow as cold as the objects they handle. She can't feel her wrists. She picks up a floral skirt, a salmon housedress, a plaid men's shirt. Back at the flat, she sits in a chair and cuts a sleeve from the man's plaid shirt, ripping along the seam. The window is open, and a few cars pass by. Two children, perhaps, laugh in echoes as they ride their bicycles through the damp autumn air.

She has already visited the Old Windsor library, the red brick building with its blue door, and it is too early yet to call her children in the United States, so she quilts. She snips at strangers' clothing and sews hexagons into flowers—the green plaid with a pale, blue center, the indigo housedress now surrounded by peach. Perhaps the television is on. Perhaps the radio. Perhaps she has already had lunch and now listens to *Woman's Hour* on BBC Radio 4. It doesn't matter. She continues her small, endless stitches until the days pass a little quicker, the old men sitting on benches in front of the corner market stop staring at her, and she and grandpa pack their suitcases to go home.

In the summer of 2009, I visit my grandparents in Missouri, where they move after Utah in search of a less expensive, less populated area. Their new living room consists of the same wooden armchairs with blue floral cushions, the same cream couch, and the same watercolor of a British cottage as all the others. My grandma asks me how my quilt projects are going and I say good—good, I'd been making progress. But I haven't. If I had really finished all the Sunbonnet Sue blocks I tell her I have, the quilt would span a king-sized bed instead of a nine-square-foot patch of wall.

In fact, I haven't used my sewing machine for two years. I'd been gone the previous two summers and then of course at college.

Upstairs in my bedroom at home, everything keeps a dusty vigil—the watercolors on the wall, the quilt rack, the stack of books by my bed. The few half-burnt candles and the silver candle snuffer. Tacked onto the bulletin board, three receipts have yellowed and curled until I can no longer read the print.

But my grandma hasn't been quilting much either. Usually when I visit she has three new quilts draped over the quilt rack, but this year there is only one—a quilt with twenty-four different basket blocks, each overflowing with hand-appliquéd flowers. My grandma sighs as she folds it, matching each of the corners precisely before hanging it back on the rack.

She just hasn't felt like quilting, she tells me, and it seems even the thought of sewing exhausts her. Too many unfinished projects. She isn't motivated. She hasn't joined a quilting guild in Missouri. Doesn't feel like it. Doesn't want more to do. Clouds move over the sun and the light in the room weakens.

She asks about the Grandmother's Flower Garden quilt, asks what I plan on doing with it.

"I'll finish it," I tell her, "but then we'll see."

As we leave the room, my grandma presses her left hand to her lower back—the one new sign that she has aged. I help her roll out manicotti in the kitchen and wonder why she mentioned the quilt—if she doubts I will finish it. As if it will always remain in the back of somebody's closet.

After college, I move from Minnesota to Nebraska, where I rent my first apartment: a one-bedroom unit in a complex of nine other one-bedroom units. The man above me sings in the shower. A different man in the complex across the alley walks through the parking lots in the morning with a glass of water and sprinkles the cars, as if blessing them. I watch him from my window, the shades half-drawn, and think about finishing the Grandmother's Flower

Garden quilt. I even go to the fabric store and spend two hours looking through the quilting supplies. I know I'll never finish it by hand, so I figure I'll purchase a template and some chalk, draw the pattern onto the back of the quilt, and use my sewing machine to complete the quilting. But when I spread the quilt across the living room floor the next day, the chalk keeps breaking. The moment I resharpen it, it snaps again. I hardly finish drawing half of a curve before I give up.

I leave the quilt on the floor, raw edges and all, and eat a sandwich. The man above me sings Broadway show tunes. The man across the alley flicks water on the cars. Grandma, two states away in a new senior complex, is probably working on a wall hanging. The breeze through the window flutters the raw edges of the cotton batting.

Two years later, when we move to New York, Kevin unpacks the quilt.

"What's this?" he asks from the second bedroom.

In the kitchen, I wipe my hands on my jeans, surprised by how much dust has made its way into the box of kitchen utensils. "What?" I call.

"This quilt."

The edges have unraveled a little more and begun to turn gray. The quilt has a caved-in kind of look, a bloated holding of its breath, as if it's asphyxiating itself. "Oh that. It's the quilt. The one my grandma gave me to finish. You know."

He furrows his eyebrows. "No, I don't think I've seen it before."

"No? I'd swear you have. I've had it forever."

"Nope, never seen it." He pokes at it with his fingers, jabbing a little.

I shrug, suddenly realizing that I've been lugging the quilt around just as long as my grandma—maybe even to the same amount of states. I pause. "Well, there it is. Just stick it somewhere in the closet," I say.

But that winter I keep thinking about the quilt. In the evenings, the temperature in the apartment drops to fifty-eight degrees and we shiver under blankets on the futon, too cold to run to the kitchen at the teakettle's shrill whistle. We can't get home for the holidays, and when we do manage to get time off and scrounge up the money to purchase plane tickets, our flight is delayed an entire day due to snow, and it seems we hardly touch down in Minneapolis when we are back at the airport, laying our bags of toiletries in gray tubs, unlacing our boots.

I work days and Kevin works both days and nights, and in the evenings I can see the lights from the highway a half mile away, and I worry that the roads will ice by the time his shift ends or that the car won't start when the temperature slips below zero, and when sirens blare in the distance, so sharp in the night, I can't breathe. I scratch the dry skin on my back until it flakes, turn on the radio, the television, all the apartment's lights, then feel silly and turn them all off. I open the closet door.

The quilt is wrinkled, but my grandma's safety pins and basting have held. I clear the kitchen table, lay the quilt on top and smooth it. Slowly, the quilt unclenches its fists and begins to soften beneath my fingers. I drape one end over my left shoulder and guide the other end beneath the foot of the machine. I mean to follow a meander pattern, with its series of loops and curves that turn in on themselves, like oak leaves, and somehow end up where the pattern begins, but the fabric won't listen. The quilt jerks to the left, then right, disrupting the smooth curve of stitches with jagged angles and intersecting lines. At first I stop and rip out the errors—start the pattern anew—but the quilt only resists with more force. Again a jagged angle, a cross where there should have been a curve. Eventually, I give in, let my hands and the needle and the heavy weight of the quilt do what they want—head in one direction, change their minds, get caught in the middle of a circle and escape by running to the left. The little light on the machine glows, the radio switches to "easy listening jazz." A soft baritone eases into the room, onto the weight on my shoulders, my lap, into the tightened knots of muscles and eyebrow, until everything becomes vowels and shadows and the soft thrum of the machine.

By the time Kevin's keys click in the back door, the machine is quiet—the foot down, the needle imbedded in cloth. I unbunch the fabric in my lap. The sometimes-curving, sometimes-jagged stitch has made its way across the entire quilt top, stitching the layers together, and then returned two inches to the left of where I'd begun.

For a moment, as Kevin's keys jiggle and the radio spits its late-night, no-program static into the room, I just stare and blink. Then, I lift the machine's foot and cut the thread.

For years, I have thought about quilting, and movement, and the landscapes I love from Minnesota. I have sensed a connection—my grandma's loneliness somehow tied with my experience of that land: the glimpse of Lake Superior from the overlooks we climbed to so much like the glimpse of my grandma's houses as we visited and then drove away.

I have sat in our office, rereading the pages Mary Alice Hansen writes about my family, stopping every now and then to study the map of the Boundary Waters that Kevin and I hung above the desk. The finished Grandmother's Flower Garden quilt is draped on the chair behind me, and in the closet sit the four plastic tubs containing my grandmother's fabric: plaids and florals, 1930s feed sack fabric, pale cotton, bright flannel left over from Christmas presents my grandma made us ten years before. I had expected the quilt and my use of the fabric to fulfill some part of my longing—to ease my grandma's isolation—but they still make me sad. If I dig deep enough, I can smell the fabric softener I associate with my grandmother's house in Dakota. When Kevin asks to move the tubs to the attic, I say no.

Mary Alice Hansen writes that my grandparents left Sawbill when my grandfather got the job in England.

I reread the lines, but they do not change. My grandmother began quilting after she moved to England for my grandpa's job, a job that, according to Hansen if not my grandmother, is why they left Sawbill to begin with.

The connection is so simple. Yes, of course, I think. Of course she would have left Sawbill for England. I ignore all the moves that came before Sawbill—Kentucky, Iowa, Missouri, Minnesota—and it becomes just that: the loss of Sawbill is the catalyst for everything that would come after, including the teenage and twenty-year-old me, lugging fabric from apartment to apartment as if warm quilts and bright colors could make a place a home.

Nonetheless, I sometimes wonder if I imagine my grandmother's loneliness and make of it something it's not. Kevin has left for work and I am sitting in the study, staring at the worn, wood floors, the now-finished quilt, and it is so easy to imagine her doing the same at the assisted living complex. Grandma holds a cup of tea or coffee, looks at the sky, and waits for some sense of what to do with her day.

But in reality she might be perfectly content. "I don't know where the time has gone," she writes, describing choir rehearsals, quilting tasks, her work at the complex's gift shop. "So sorry it took so long to reply."

No pining. No wishing for earlier, more settled days.

If I asked her if she was happy, she might say yes.

Or she might say no.

Which is why I don't ask.

Another photograph: a montage made my junior year of high

school, after my last visit to Dakota, by superimposing a landscape over a self-portrait. In the portrait, I sit in a chair in my bedroom, one arm resting across my lap, the other on the armrest. I do not look at the camera but at my hand, which touches a red- and blue-squared quilt my grandma made. Behind that, in the landscape: the bluff nearest my grandma's house. The image is faint, but it is there—a silhouette of trees across my chest, an outline of rock along the folds of the quilt.

MOVEMENT

🌿 I NEVER KNEW my grandparents when they lived on the North Shore. I never even visited the North Shore with my grandparents. Unlike my maternal relatives, who would occasionally rent a cabin near Tofte, where we'd play card games, visit the waterfalls at nearby state parks, and take family photographs with all of the cousins, my paternal grandparents never vacationed with us. We visited them at their houses, and they visited us at our home, but that was that.

Looking back, it is strange to think of my obsession with Sawbill, the way it is intertwined with my relationship with my grandparents—the two inseparable even though I have no memories of my grandparents on the North Shore.

Yet whenever I mention an upcoming trip north, my grandma says she wishes she could get back up there once more, at least to see how everything has changed.

"I'll let you know how it looks," I tell her before Kevin and I go to the Boundary Waters. And later, before I head to Grand Marais for research, "I'll take pictures."

"I'd like that," she says.

After Utah my grandparents move to Missouri. They move from their adobe home with the red-tiled roof to a one-level ranch in Web City, just outside of Joplin. The homes in their neighborhood are large and new. They boast brick facades and two- and three-car garages. Children play basketball from their driveways and ride their bikes around the six streets. But the neighborhood is far enough away from Joplin and the other nearby cities that cows graze just a few blocks from the subdivision. The narrow streets lack shoulders and sometimes even curbs. When we first drive in, my father clutches the steering wheel in the dark. "Where is this place?" my mother says.

I visit the house near Joplin two or three times. One time, my two young cousins and aunt from Montana come too, and we spend the evening filling up air mattresses that we spread around the living room floor. My grandparents' miniature dachshund and my parents' German Shepherd/Husky mix chase each other, nipping at each other's ears, sharing bones, wagging their tails, as if there wasn't a sixty-pound difference between them. We go on long walks around the neighborhood, taking the same streets again and again. My grandma points out the road signs that teenagers keep stealing—signs such as "James Street" and "Kelly Avenue." One night, when the neighbors have all the lights in their house on and my grandma wants to see what the inside of their house looks like, we take a walk through the backyards of the houses around us.

"What ugly wallpaper," she says. "Though I do like those couches. And look at that ceiling fan. Their living area has a better floor plan than ours."

Dew has formed on the grass and wets my sandals. The moon barely illuminates the grills and patio furniture we maneuver around. I hold my breath and watch for movement from the windows. I wonder out loud if we should go back.

"No one will see us," my grandma says. "It's dark. Let's look at that house too."

And so in my strongest memory of Web City, I follow my grandma down the line of backyards, that small dip where they meet each other.

When I move to Lincoln, Nebraska, I live closer to my grandparents than any of my other relatives, though I am still six hours away by car. That fall, my grandma stocks the refrigerator with sandwiches and the freezer with chicken pot pies for my grandpa and then drives north to visit me. I take her to the quilt museum and then to the farmer's market, where we sample cheese and bread. My grandma purchases a watermelon, which we spend half an hour trying to cut open in my kitchen. I own five IKEA knives, each as dull as the next. We wedge the largest knife into the top of the watermelon, seesaw it back and forth until it begins to cut into the fruit. But soon the knife is stuck, the cheap metal bending between the weight of the watermelon's sides.

"We need to get you new knives," my grandma says, huffing, one hand on the handle of the knife, one on the top of the blade.

"Let me try," I say, but still the knife won't cut into the fruit. It stops a third of the way in, silver edge gleaming as the pink juice dribbles onto the wooden cutting board. "I guess so!" I say, and we laugh.

My grandmother grew up in a one-room apartment. She shared a bed with her sister and mom. She never celebrated Christmas until she married, and now, as we eat the sawed watermelon and a spinach quiche, she asks what I want in her will.

"I know your brother wants the painting of the dog. I've penciled his name on the back. But is there anything you want?"

I use my fork to maneuver the crust of my quiche into the residue of salad dressing. I snap the crust into two and take a bite.

"Your grandpa and I are thinking of moving. The house is too big to keep up. I don't want to sell anything valuable, or anything you'd like to keep."

I nod, force my lips into a half smile—what I hope looks empathetic. "No, nothing particular," I say. "Just a quilt, maybe. I'd take a quilt."

The comment rests there between us, as if a quilt could capture all these movements and migrations and piece them together until they're complete.

My grandma leaves the next morning before dawn. She drives down 16th Street into darkness, the taillights of her car red dots that fade into black. Back in my apartment, I turn on lights and put away blankets. Still, the apartment feels suddenly empty—the space in the bathroom where she put her make-up, the curve of the pillow where she laid her head.

Once the sun rises, I walk toward campus just to get outside the apartment. The fountains near the state capital fill the air with chlorine. Yellow locust leaves slip into the cracks of sidewalks. It will rain soon. I roll my sleeves down from the elbows as aluminum cans scrape against the ground. The sky darkens toward the west and pedestrians walk quicker, but what do I have to return to? Rooms with open windows? Quilts long grown cool?

I sit on a bench as the wind hits my face. I am not sad, but rather apathetic with waiting, with the emptiness of this place.

The next year, my grandparents move from Joplin to a senior housing facility forty miles east in Marionville, Missouri. They move because the house near Joplin has gotten too difficult to maintain. Grandpa has had trouble with his vision and can no longer drive. The house near Joplin was too far away from everything—shopping, doctors, restaurants. In Marionville, they buy a small "cottage" and eat lunches at the complex's dining area. They go to Wii bowling tournaments and play bingo on Fridays. My grandpa meets some of the other men once a week to play pool and discuss politics. I've never seen him so social. And so, even though the move surprises me—they'd only been near Joplin for a few years—when I e-mail my grandma I tell her it sounds like a great place. It sounds like it is good for them.

I am the first of my family to visit their new home. On Labor Day weekend I pack up the car and take off, driving southeast through Nebraska until I make it to the Missouri River, where I cross for a short stretch into Iowa. The land here, aside from the mellow bluffs near the Missouri, is flat and filled with corn. Dust hovers over the roads and intersections. Trucks and semis whiz past my small car. I pop an audiobook into the CD player and adjust the volume.

I do not know what to make of this region. In Lincoln, I like best the old warehouse district, which sits next to the train tracks and houses art galleries, coffee shops, a licorice store, and an independent bookstore. Sometimes, I write on the balcony of one of the coffee shops and look at the Amtrak station, the line of six railroad tracks, and feel the roads vibrate ever so slightly when a train moves through. If only this were a river, I think. If only this part of the city overlooked water. I've found myself thinking more and more of northeast Minnesota. The lakes and the trees. The bunchberry and alder. Lincoln is all sky—wind moving between buildings, dust from the west making its way through the screens of my windows and now coating the sides of my car. How strange to visit family by driving south.

I pass the Joplin exit and turn onto another highway, which will take me forty minutes east toward Marionville. Billboards promote an endless stream of "gentlemen clubs" and "adult video stores," a fact that gives my trip and my drive a sense of despondence. I am entering something gritty, something swept under a rug—a feeling that doesn't entirely leave when I pull into the senior housing facility. The air in the community rooms smells of old age and mold. The books in the lending library have yellowed on the edges, much like the tiled floors in the assisted living complex and nursing home.

Nonetheless, my grandpa enjoys showing me off. "How do you do?" he asks each resident when we stop for lunch the next day. "Have you met our granddaughter?" Dietary aides serve orange Jell-O salad, mashed potatoes topped with a thick gravy, and two choices of pie. After lunch, my grandfather joins some of the men in the rec room for a game of pool. A neighbor drives him back to his cottage after. In the passenger seat of the neighbor's minivan, my grandfather looks small, shrunken, and gray.

"This seems like a nice place," I tell my grandma, though it is hard for me to see them there: the plastic drinking glasses, the beep of oxygen tanks and scuttle of walkers. She points out the gift shop, where postcards have curled from humidity and lack of use. She points out the snack area, where residents can always get soft-serve ice cream and powdery cappuccino. Then we get into the car to tour the city. As we drive, the places my grandparents have lived in the past few years arrange themselves in a gallery between us— each place less homelike to me than the others. St. George, Utah, with its red grit and sand; Web City, Missouri, with its isolated homes and shoulderless roads; and now Marionville, where the only real novelty is the white squirrels some of the residents feed. Otherwise, the city contains two gas stations, one grocery store, and a downtown square of boarded up windows, weeds sprouting from washed-out sidewalks. Where is the energy of the lake, the bluffs?

I want to ask why they keep moving and if she wishes she could stay put. I want to know where she would have preferred to stay put—and I want her answer to be in one of her homes in

Minnesota. But all I can ask, as we return to the cottage and I help cut tomatoes for dinner, is what home she liked best.

"Oh, the farmhouse in Ankeny, Iowa," she says, opening a can of olives for taco salad. "It had such beautiful woodwork."

The following January, my dad and I drive down to Marionville to visit. My father picks me up in Lincoln, and even though he's already driven six hours, he doesn't let me take the wheel. Like me, he tends to get carsick when a passenger. But unlike me, he isn't content to stare out of windows.

The same farm fields pass before us. We cross the Missouri River three times, looping around Kansas City. My dad asks about school, and I say it is going fine. He flips to the local NPR station. The miles pass. I've begun to read about "place"—what makes people keep moving while others stay put. I've read essays and books by Scott Russell Sanders, who writes in *Staying Put,*

> Wholesale dis-placement may be inevitable; but we should not suppose that it occurs without disastrous consequences for the earth and for ourselves. People who root themselves in places are likelier to know and care for those places than are people who root themselves in ideas. When we cease to be migrants and become inhabitants, we might begin to pay enough heed and respect to where we are. By settling in, we have a chance of making a durable home for ourselves, our fellow creatures, and our descendants.

I've read Greta Gaard, whose own quest for such placeness, a quest that takes her across multiple states, ends with the personal realization that to feel at home she must continually create and recreate relationships with the people and environments around her. "According to water, home is not a static place or destination, not a noun but a verb, a process of creating relationships to place, to creatures, and to people. Being at home means accepting impermanence, entering fully into the cycles of life, stepping into the flow of relationships, a movement of energy, a dance of creation, preservation, dissolution, and re-creation." Her ultimate conclusion unnerves me. I want her to reiterate Sanders's claims, but she does not.

As my dad and I travel, I flip through a stack of books I've brought by Aldo Leopold, Wendell Berry, and Barry Lopez—outdoor enthusiasts like me and my family, but people who have nurtured a sense of place. People who have spent their careers advocating a kind of local knowledge. I am entranced by the stability and lifestyles of these writers. I want to garden, to have a compost pile, to know the names of the trees and the plants and the birds. I want to make one small parcel of earth cleaner, less toxic, but how can I do that when I, and my family, keep moving?

My dad tells me his university has decided to cut his department. He is applying for jobs and has an interview in St. Croix. "It could be a neat opportunity," he says in the car.

I run my hand along the shoulder strap of my seatbelt and then press my fists into my stomach. An all-too-familiar hollowness plummets to my gut, pulling everything inward. We will lose ourselves. We will become Sanders's displaced sightseers, drifting alone without community or kin. A cold sweat washes over my forehead. I close my eyes and force myself to swallow.

I know my dad's trying to hold us together financially—to provide for my mom, my siblings, and me. Yet as the highway rumbles beneath us and the miles on the odometer roll, my desire for a different heritage—a different life for us all—grows and grows and grows.

My dad and I stop for coffee again, then dinner. Shortly after dusk, we pull into my grandparents' cottage, where the front door opens for us and my grandparents envelop us in the conversation of the lonely, the bored.

"There was this guy—what was his name, Helen?" my grandpa begins.

"John?"

"John. Yes, that's right. John Little, the local sheriff, and probably the only black man in all of Cook County. But he was a great guy—had the best stories. He sure was fun to talk to. He'd come over to the resort some evenings just to talk and see how things were going."

"Sometimes he'd come by for coffee," my grandma adds.

"Yes, that's right."

"Or dinner."

"Yes, but anyway, he'd come by and tell us the county news or how many bears were out by the landfill, and there were always some. That was a sight."

"Do you need anything?" My grandma stands, one hand on the back of a chair. "Coffee? Cheesecake? I just picked up a turtle cheesecake. It's thawing in the fridge . . ."

My dad and I shake our heads.

"Are you sure? I can make a pot of decaf." She steps toward the kitchen.

"No, that's fine," my dad says as I cover a yawn.

"Steve," she says, almost in a reprimand.

"Really. I'm fine. Still full from dinner."

My grandma sighs and sits back down.

"Anyway," my grandpa says from the couch, and as he pats their dachshund beneath a blanket, the weariness of travel lulls me, and I turn to the story. "He always wanted one of those bears."

E-MAIL FROM GRANDMA

✿ IN LATE JULY 2011, the first full summer Kevin and I live in upstate New York, my grandparents move from their retirement home in Marionville, Missouri, to Springfield, Missouri. "I just got your e-mail and thanks for the good wishes on our move Thursday. I will be glad when this move is over with and we are settled in. It has been a long wait," my grandma writes. She titles her e-mail "Sawbill" in response to a query I sent a few days before, an e-mail in which I asked for specifics: dates, daily tasks, anything that would make her experience there real for me.

As my grandma moves from one retirement home to another, I am collecting material. I am asking for photographs and fanning them out on the office floor. When I think of Sawbill, it is an air bubble in my throat. It is a family heirloom that we have lost from neglect or thievery, but something I want to reclaim.

"We purchased the lodge in 1972, I think," my grandma writes. "And we let it go back to the original owner around 1976. We would have kept it but the Forest Service would not let me know if they would renew the lease, which would have expired in a few years. Also they wanted the one cabin we had winterized as a ranger station, so they really didn't want the resort there."

My grandma's paragraphs are thick with text. I imagine her at her computer, typing with quick fingers, occasionally pausing to press at her lower back.

> The Lodge itself was huge. You could almost stand up in the fireplaces. We had the dining room, lounge, kitchen, office, employee room, and reception office in it. There were no phones. Since we were 25 miles in from Lake Superior we had to go to Tofte nearly every day for supplies. The businesses we purchased from would leave the supplies in a shed that was by the store there. We would take turns with the outfitters on trips down to the shore. [. . .] In 1957 Frank and Mary Alice Hansen, who had been going to Sawbill for years, took over the outfitting from Jean Raiken. That was too bad for the Lodge in a way, as the outfitting was the money maker there. They moved the outfitting from the Lodge area closer to the boat landing on Sawbill Lake.

In the same paragraph, my grandma offers her explanation for the loss of the lodge: "We made our payments all the time we were there and also paid the real estate taxes while we had it. However, Jean did not pay the past taxes on it, which she was supposed to do according to the agreement we had. So anyway, we let it go back to her. I think another couple did take it over but eventually it went back to its natural state, and in 1983 or 1984 Solbakken Resort in Lutsen purchased the Lodge at an auction and moved it log by log to their place on Lake Superior. I think they use it in their advertising, but they have changed it a lot in the inside."

In her second hefty paragraph, my grandma describes the people she met at the resort. She has mentioned some of them before, when I've asked her questions in person, but now they arrange themselves in a list: symphony orchestra members from Louisville, Kentucky; a couple from the Finger Lakes in New York; businessmen from Chicago; a lawyer and his family from Duluth; a busload of people from the University of Minnesota; scout troops; an older couple from Davenport, Iowa—the man, my grandma says, had a recording studio in his home. His wife "had the cutest giggle and told me she didn't dust in her house because if an antique dish or item was missing she would know it."

My grandma follows her description with the following two sentences: "It was long hours for me at the resort. Five in the morning until sometimes after midnight." She explains that she "would go to the resort the first of May each year and go back home October 1." During the winter, she says she worked her "regular job" in the Twin Cities, where she did administrative work and conducted audits.

I reread the sentences. I hadn't heard of my grandma's workload before. If my family had kept the resort, and I had helped run it, could I really work that long? Could I devote my entire summer to the business?

Later in the e-mail: "The Forest Service also wanted us to put holding tanks in for the septic, but I had the State [Department] out and they said as long as everything was working okay there was no need to do that. It would have been a huge expense."

My grandmother has always been a stubborn and particular shopper. When I go grocery shopping with her, she tests each grape between her fingers, squeezing them to make sure they have the appropriate give. She'll go to multiple stores to find the best prices, and I've rarely heard her praise a restaurant. Usually she says, "that was disappointing" or "could have been better." It is easy to imagine her on the phone with the Forest Service, calling in the state for a second opinion on the septic system.

It is easy to imagine her and Mary Alice Hansen arguing about business. It is easy to imagine her frustration with the then-aging Jean Raiken.

After a short paragraph in which my grandmother mentions the wine tastings at the new retirement home and asks about my siblings and my summer job, she mentions Mary Alice.

> There is a book written by Mary Alice Hansen called "Sawbill." Your dad told me he has a copy of it. So maybe you could get his copy and it would give you some information. I am going to go to Barnes & Noble and get the book, as I'd like to see it. Also your Dad might be able to give you some stories of the resort. He and Lori spent the summers there with me. Mark worked there in the summer too. We always had to watch out for bears. Mark shot one not very far from the Lodge. He had the fur in a rug for a long time. I don't know what he ever did with it. One time a bear got through the window in the kitchen and got his head caught in the hole where we kept the garbage can that we used when we cleared the dishes. Also a moose went through the Lodge roof one winter. These two things didn't happen when we had the resort though.

I smile at this paragraph—the odd juxtaposition of information as well as the belated remark about the bear and the moose. *These two things didn't happen when we had the resort though.* But my grandma's words also raise questions. When did my dad tell my grandma that he had Mary Alice's book? When did he purchase it?

The stories don't line up with what I know of my father, so much white space and emptiness between those lines—just like the quick ending to my grandma's e-mail immediately after: "Guess it is bed-time now. Maybe more later. Lots of Love, Grandma."

I save the e-mail in my inbox for a year before copying and pasting it into a Word document. The jumble of facts and stories are difficult to dismantle. I stare at the large blocks of text, the problematic dates, the long working hours. What actually happened? Why did they leave? What does my father remember?

ST. CROIX

WHEN KEVIN AND I book flights for St. Croix, we do so with hesitancy. It fits too closely the sort of places other newlyweds go—the sandy beaches and blue water, the thatched roofs of boardwalk bars, the promenades where vendors sell sunglasses and floral dresses. If Kevin and I were to list the places we want to visit, we'd list destinations like Alaska, Maine, and Ireland—cooler climates where we can wear jackets and our lips will grow chapped in the cold. St. Croix—or any island in the Caribbean—wouldn't even appear at the bottom.

But St. Croix is where my parents have moved—my father two years ago and my mother one year after. It is where they have settled temporarily now that my siblings and I have all moved out. They have offered to fly Kevin and me there, and I am curious to see how St. Croix has changed them. When they flew back to Minnesota for Christmas, my mother, like my father the year before, blasted the heat. Each morning, I found my suddenly bronzed parents in front of the gas fireplace, their shoulders hunched as they rubbed their arms with their hands.

"It's so cold!" my mom said, while my father, who had kept the thermostat at a strict sixty-eight degrees when I was in high school, pushed it to seventy-two. He refused to wear socks with his sandals, and his toes turned blue when he walked barefoot on the floor.

"It's eighty-four in St. Croix," he told me as I poured a mug of coffee. "Next Christmas, we should spend it there."

I still do not know what to do with my father's joy, his sudden love of the tropics. Two years ago now, when he first flew to St. Croix for a job interview, he spoke of the boardwalk where you could see fish the size of a snowboard. He spoke of the mahimahi he ate for dinner, the fish tacos at the beachside pub. When he returned, he bought us all dolphin-shaped air fresheners for our cars and started ordering books about the Virgin Islands. My mother frowned. "I don't know. It's awfully far." But my father was decided. He'd worked ten years for the local university; once they cut his department, he needed a new job. "The students there are eager to learn," he said. "We can sail and go snorkeling. It'll be an adventure."

So my father left, and the next year my mother joined him, and now, in March of 2011, Kevin and I visit over our spring break. When we leave our apartment for the airport at 5:00 a.m., I am uneasy, slightly nauseous. Even though my parents paid for our plane tickets as a wedding present, the tickets themselves cost more than Kevin and I make in a month. I, who spend two hours a week balancing our meager checking account, don't think we deserve a spring break vacation. Newlyweds in our financial situation, I think, should not travel like this.

But I am anxious to see my parents, and after a long first winter in New York, the burst of green and the heat come as a relief. "Welcome!" my dad says, while my mother grins from inside the car.

As we drive to the condo, my father points out the university he now works at, the restaurants they've been to. He winds through the mountain pass in the center of the island and then sweeps along the coast toward Christiansted.

"Don't mind this part," my mom says as we make our way through a stretch of crumbling buildings, bars with boarded windows, and a church soup kitchen where men in ragged jeans sleep in the shade. The unemployment rate in the US Virgin Islands is double that of the states, and here it shows. "I wish the main street didn't go through this section," my mom says. She hasn't taken to the island the way my dad has. A few weeks ago she called me to say that she was moving back to Minnesota in the summer. She wanted to resume her teaching job at the local elementary school; St. Croix just wasn't for her. Since that decision, she's been counting down the days until Kevin and I visit; it will give her something to do.

We drive past an eighteenth-century fort and up a hill. Behind us, the steep hills of the island fall into the sea. My dad pulls onto a side road and into a residential complex. "Here we are!" he says, parking in front of a line of condos, off-white with red-tile roofs and wrought-iron decorations that cover the doors and windows. An iguana rests on a retaining wall. A yellow and green succulent sends spikes into the air.

Everything feels strange and slightly unreal: the wicker couch and chairs in the living room, the plates that screech when scraped with a fork, the ants that congregate around the slightest trace of sugar. These are not images I associate with my parents—my father who used to collect thick winter sweaters, my mother whose face reddens at the slightest heat. Now they wear lightweight linen. The rooms hum with fans. I keep my lips tight, my eyes wide. I grip the strap of my backpack as I try to absorb all that I see. From the living room and kitchen windows, the lagoon opens to ocean, where sailboats and catamarans glint in the sun. Kevin and I drop our bags off in the guest bedroom and walk, silent, to the kitchen, where my mom offers us iced tea. I hold the glass, feel the unfamiliarity of it all on my fingers. I am new here, but my parents are not. Their lives have continued without me.

My mother is excited to show us around the island. She knows we will enjoy the historical sites, so she has made an itinerary for each day my dad works. Early in the week, she takes us to an old sugarcane plantation that now functions as a museum. We meander through the grounds and then make our way up to the house for the start of the tour.

At a table just before the stairs to the veranda, two Cruzan women sit in the shade. One, maybe in her forties or fifties, with damp stains beneath her armpits and skin that wants to pop from her button-up shirt, fans herself, collecting tickets. The other, a woman in her late twenties, has pulled her hair back so tight it silhouettes her round face. They speak to each other in the local dialect—bulbous sounds I cannot understand. I eavesdrop on their vowels, their consonants, and wonder what they think of all the middle-aged couples from England and the United States, tourists who take pictures of the architecture and the chickens running through the yard. I want to understand what these women think. I want to know which tourists they make fun of, and what they think of someone like me.

When the younger woman stands up and says in Standard English that the tour will begin soon, the clarity of her speech surprises me. She smiles to the crowd, smoothing the skirt on her thighs. Her teeth are slightly yellow, the front one crooked by a few degrees. Yet she walks erect, her body built like the palm trees that grow near the beach. She sweeps her arms to point out the building's nine-foot doorway, the empty moat dug to keep the lower level cool. When a tourist in her seventies complains of the heat and her husband almost sits in a roped-off chair, the guide just smiles, nods as if at a joke, and asks the man to please not sit down. Her composure strikes me.

"Come through this room," she says. "See how tall the windows are? The circular shape of the room? Even without fans or air conditioning, the room stays cool. And note the mahogany end tables and chairs. Built on the islands. You can't find that kind of wood anymore."

She moves to the bedroom, refurnished with a double bed, a bassinet, and a large wardrobe. She points toward a mahogany chair with armrests that extend well past the seat. "This is a planter's chair," she says. "Here, the plantation owner would rest his feet from the fields. Once the swelling went down, he could take off his boots."

A middle-aged man touches the extended armrest.

"Go ahead," the tour guide says. "People like to try it out. This is a replication, not an original. See," she says, pointing to a group of photographs taped to a wall, "people like to feel what it is like to sit in a planter's chair. Go ahead. Take a photograph."

Sure enough, most of the visitors try out the chair. Two young kids clamber on as their parents take a picture. The husband of the seventy-something-year-old woman chuckles as he lowers himself into the seat.

"Want to?" Kevin asks, but I shake my head. It feels wrong—all these tourists trying out the planter's chair. Pretending, for a moment, to have been the Danish owners of the plantation—to have spent all day in the sugarcane fields, overseeing the Caribbean slaves. I wonder how long the tour guide's family has lived here—if she is descended from slaves or if her family came to the island later. And if her ancestors were Afro-Indian natives who fought in the 1800s revolts, how terrible it must be to work at this plantation, to guide tourists through these rooms every day.

But maybe she majored in museum studies, like Kevin. Maybe

this is a job she really loves. She has a stake in this location, this history, that I cannot fathom. The fact silences me.

"You don't want to try it?" the tour guide asks, once everyone but my mom, Kevin, and I have sat in the chair.

"No thanks," I say, standing on the outside of the group, a temporary visitor who does not belong.

On Wednesday morning I wake up early and join my father for coffee. I take out the Sudoku daily puzzles I've brought, and my father, who owns the same calendar of puzzles, challenges me to a race. Coffee sends steam toward the ceiling, and a wave of heat rushes across my face. But still we drink from our mugs and hunch over our puzzles, jotting numerals in the small boxes. My father wins, as always, but I finish close behind. A respectable defeat. Sailboats move across the lagoon and the ceiling fan pushes wafts of air to the corners of the room. A beautiful day. We push our puzzles aside. Though my mom was the one to complain of the distance, in his own way, I know my father has missed us.

My dad lifts his mug to his lips and slurps softly. "It was a mistake for your mom not to work this year," he tells me, his voice quiet. "She was too bored." He tells me how, over the months, the things she doesn't like have started to bother her more—from long lines at the post office to the unreliable cable TV. She hasn't taken to St. Croix in the same way he has. "She needed more to keep her busy," he says.

I imagine my mom alone in the apartment all day while my dad teaches on campus. She'd walk to the pool, or maybe down to Christiansted, where she'd read at the coffee shop and meander through the stores. I imagine the endless days in the eighties, the boredom as she clicks through books on the Kindle. Although she had wanted to take a year off—to have time to relax and help me in the fall with the wedding—how strange it must have been for her without structure. She'd raised us and taught elementary school since she was twenty years old, but now she was stuck in the heat without family, friends, coworkers, or purpose—just the children's book she said she wanted to write, the summer dress she wanted to find. Whenever I called her on Sundays, she often said she hadn't done anything exciting. "Just the same old," she'd tell me, later complaining of the slow pace of life and the high poverty levels.

My dad sighs and takes a final gulp from his coffee. "Oh well," he says, with a half smile. I remember his dreams when he first accepted the job. He wanted to go sailing, to buy a boat. The night before, when we had dinner near the marina, he pointed out the ideal size—a nineteen-foot blue and white sailboat bobbing off the pier. In fact, the whole point of taking the job in St. Croix was to enjoy island life, to slow down his pace and relax. But I know he's taken on side teaching jobs to keep them afloat as my mom took the year off—to pay for our plane tickets, to support my sister still in school, and to fund part of my wedding. With his work schedule and my mom's boredom, their evenings must have stretched and shriveled.

My dad fills his mug with more coffee. "Need more?" he asks.

I shake my head. I ache for both of them. Their isolation. And though I don't think Kevin and I will ever decide to live apart, haven't we, too, already made choices that take us away from family, from the places we love?

"Well, I suppose I should get back to work."

As my dad swivels his chair toward his desk, my neck prickles with heat.

On Thursday my mom drops my Dad off at campus and then takes Kevin and me to Frederiksted, on the other side of the thirty-mile island. We drive past fruit stands where native Cruzans sell plantains and other produce from tables along a gravel turnoff. We drive past low-income housing where hurricane shutters slit into dark rooms. Up in the hills, the white and pastel mansions with three- or four-car garages form light blotches of paint on the green slopes. That is where the millionaires live—the Americans and Europeans who come here on vacation.

Frederiksted boasts a harbor deep enough for cruise ships, so the boardwalk is lined with small stores and grassy lawns where locals set up as vendors. Today, there aren't any cruise ships, and most of the stores are closed. At first, it seems the only people outside are the homeless men in their thin, khaki shorts and stained, buttonless shirts. They slump in the shade of palm trees, one cacao-colored hand on a ratty backpack, another on a cardboard sign requesting food. They look up when we pass, briefly animated by our shadows. "Spare change?" they say. "I've been out of work for two years." I feel their eyes on my back, but when I turn around, they have already slumped onto the ground.

We enter my mother's favorite café—a brightly painted green and pink room facing the ocean. We eat sandwiches served with fresh slices of pineapple and then tour an old fort. The red paint chips on the pentagon-shaped walls. Decade-old posters about slavery and island life fade in the darkened back rooms. Once we've circled the fort, we walk out onto the pier until the water deepens, obscuring the bottom. Frederiksted shrinks behind us—a long line of pastel buildings with hurricane shutters and white trim.

"I'm glad we're here," I tell my mom.

"I'm so glad you are, too," she replies.

When my father first moved to St. Croix, my mom had admitted that she feared she and my dad would begin moving as often as my grandparents. "I don't want to do that," my mom had said. The comment had troubled me because I worried about the same thing. Now, I wonder what will happen next year, when my mom returns to Minnesota alone. What will happen the year after, when my dad has said he will look for a new job?

My mom sighs. "I wish you both could stay longer."

I adjust my sunglasses and lift my face into the sun. "Me too. The week is going so fast."

We look for coconuts under palm trees. We squint into the horizon and search for large boats.

"It's too bad this opportunity didn't come later," my mom says, "when your dad and I were closer to retiring. I don't like the idea of being so far away when you start a family." She adjusts her purse on her shoulder.

Toward the middle of the island, the hills rise up, steep and green. Though Kevin and I aren't planning on having a child anytime soon, my mom's comment nonetheless unsettles me. I try not to think of the future, when my siblings, parents, and I might very well live in four different states.

That evening we pick up my dad from the university and drive to the Christiansted boardwalk for fish tacos and the monthly art walk. Caucasian gallery owners hold court behind front desks while new retirees in thin summer dresses and linen suits sip wine and admire work by continental US artists who've traveled to the area. Across the rooms, other tourists with small backpacks and passport holders point out photographs. The light posts glow yellow on the buildings. Whispers carry up into the night. In a gallery with paintings of sea turtles so detailed that overfilling landfills reflect in their eyes, a group of six wealthy tourists discuss where they'll dock their yachts during hurricane season. One thinks he might try St. Kitts this time around. Another generally stays near St. Thomas, but he's heard Trinidad is nice.

I eavesdrop on the group and cringe. So many of my dad's university students here have never left the thirty-mile island, yet tonight the streets fill with wealthy tourists who travel purely for recreation. I resist being associated with such groups. Instead, I want to blend in with the locals, to know the names of the trees and the flowers. If I knew the history, I'd be less apt to make mistakes—to become complicit in a system I'd otherwise critique.

Yet here I am, with my sandals and sunglasses and my shoulder bag. I've come from New York for a week and I am taking in the sights, as my parents have all year. Colonialism and postcolonialism: a knot I cannot unravel, and perhaps it is just the visibility of it all that makes me uncomfortable. In Minnesota, the history of displacement is hidden. The Boundary Waters has been set aside as a wilderness area, involving permits and rules, a fact that erases the complicated relations between the Chippewa and Cree, the Ojibwa and voyageurs, the loggers and miners. It's equally problematic, but somehow softer. Here, on the other hand, mansions tower over government housing and the mostly white tourists contrast starkly with the Cruzan natives.

I wonder why my father came to St. Croix. For so long he had dreamt of owning a cabin in northern Minnesota. On camping trips, he'd pick up real estate booklets at grocery stores and gas stations. We'd spend rainy evenings in tents searching for the perfect cabin—something with a nice loft where everyone could sleep and perhaps even running water in the kitchen. For years, I wanted to share that dream with him. I drew cabin floor plans in old notebooks, and when Kevin and I started camping up north, I looked at cabin listings and collected the same booklets.

But now my father wants a boat. He wants to sail from St. Croix to Florida. He is tan and fit, and he is happy in this place where our family lacks history, where our own role in cultural tensions somehow seems more fraught. Meanwhile, my mother does crossword puzzles on the wicker couch and counts down the days until she moves back to Minnesota.

There are only two more days left of our vacation. The thought makes my chest go stiff.

On Friday night, Kevin gets sick. All week he's woken up increasingly congested, but now he spikes a fever. He throws up three times in the bathroom, and his blood sugar skyrockets. I rub his back and listen for his breath. I bring him glasses of water from the kitchen.

"Do you think it's the flu?" I ask. "Food poisoning? Did you give yourself enough insulin for dinner?"

"I don't know," he whispers, pale on his pillow.

He'd had a sinus infection the week before, and we wonder if all the new pollens have aggravated his sinuses and brought it back. Nonetheless, his blood sugar levels make me nervous. If he falls into a diabetic coma, I do not know what hospital our insurance will cover. Kevin's breath comes halting and heavy. My father snores from across the hall.

"I'm sorry," Kevin whispers. "I don't think I'll be able to do much today."

"It's okay," I tell him. "Don't worry. Get some rest." But my stomach twists with anxiety. We were supposed to have a nice time with my parents, to relax after the long winter. Instead, the very air here is pushing us away.

I squeeze my eyes shut and press my head into my pillow. I don't know what to do.

Kevin wakes up and tests his blood sugar while, outside, birds I cannot name send shrill calls into the night.

Our last couple of days pass quickly. My mom and I swim at the pool while Kevin recovers. Kevin eats toast while the rest of us grill salmon. We play cribbage and do crossword puzzles and watch the sun set over the water. I try to hold onto each moment, like a small lizard cupped in my hands, but all too soon our departure date arrives. At the airport, the customs official assumes we were vacationing on St. Croix. I consider correcting her and saying we were visiting family, but I don't.

We fly from St. Croix to Puerto Rico and from Puerto Rico to Atlanta. From Atlanta we fly to Washington, DC, where we're supposed to catch our last flight to Binghamton, New York. When we arrive at the gate, the attendant informs us of maintenance problems. Two hours later, a mechanic finally shows up.

At midnight, the gate attendant allows us to board the small propeller plane. We taxi to the runway, the cabin quickly growing warm without the air conditioning. I breathe through my mouth, but still the humid stench of stained seats and other passengers crushes my face, my throat, my hands. Kevin falls asleep beside me as I gulp in air. My stomach turns. The pilot does a second safety check and then pulls the plane into a side lane. We sit on the tarmac for an hour and a half. At two in the morning, the pilot's tired voice crackles over the intercom. "I'm sorry for the wait," he says, "but a heavy storm has just passed through Binghamton. We were hoping to get the go ahead, but it looks like a heavy fog has now moved in. The visibility is too low to ensure a safe landing. We'll have to return to the gate." The passengers groan. Back at the gate, the thirty of us stagger into the florescent lighting, rolling our luggage behind us.

The airline gives us a voucher for a hotel. By the time we arrive at the hotel, we have two hours before we need to head back to the airport for our 6:00 a.m. flight. Kevin and I brush our teeth and collapse into the bed, waking an hour later.

Again, we trudge through security, my eyes bloodshot from lack of sleep, my hair disheveled since I chose fifteen more minutes in bed instead of a shower. Kevin takes out the breakfast vouchers the airline also gave us.

"Why don't we go there?" he asks, pointing to a sit-down restaurant.

"Fresh Eggs: $3.99," the sign reads.

I shake my head. "Ugh." Bile rises to my throat at the thought of food. It is 4:00 a.m. Passengers sleep sprawled over chairs, their body oil joining thousands of others to burnish the plastic. My bones ache for my own bed, where I can lay flat in the dark and not think of anything.

We walk through the almost-empty passageways in search of breakfast, passing closed vendor after closed vendor. Our backpacks dig into our shoulders. We circle the terminal and return to the gate where we started.

When the loudspeakers send out their recorded messages about passenger safety and odd-looking luggage, I grimace and cover my ears. Back in St. Croix, my parents are just getting up. Back in Binghamton, our refrigerator hums and my shampoo waits in its dispenser. Yet here we are, caught between destinations, and even worse, my parents and I have chosen this life for ourselves. We will never all return to Minnesota. From now on, our lives will be airports and flight delays, early morning alarms to go through security. The thought burns into me like the florescent lights. I touch my forehead to my knees. Though I know my parents are lucky to have this opportunity—that Kevin and I are lucky to have found work in New York—a sadness settles in my gut. I do not want to travel anywhere. I want to stay put.

ALONENESS

IN DECEMBER 2011, a friend and colleague has surgery to remove a tumor from her right breast. The month before the surgery, she is a windstorm of productivity. She grades quickly, pushes collaborative projects along until the rest of us heave, breathless, as we try to catch up. She studies with friends in the evenings and asks if anyone wants to do work at coffee shops on weekends. The day of the surgery, her mom drives one hour south to be with her. Kevin and I wish her the best and leave a card among the others in her mailbox. As I walk back to my own apartment, I wonder what would happen if Kevin and I were in her situation. What kind of support group would we have?

My mother asked the same question about herself just a few months ago, when her friend's breast cancer returned and spread. Her friend's church held spaghetti dinners and pancake breakfasts to help pay for her medical bills, and hundreds of family, friends, and coworkers chipped in to drive her to appointments and offer what support they could.

"If something like that happened to me," my mom said on the

phone that weekend, "I wouldn't get that kind of support. Not to the same magnitude."

"Sure you would," I said. "We'd do what we could."

"I know you would," my mom answered. "But I don't go to church anymore. I don't know many people here outside of work. If I had a spaghetti dinner, twenty-five people would show up."

"More would come than that," I said, though I, too, wasn't sure. I stared at the photographs of Sawbill, still stacked on the floor by my chair. I flipped through a handful without looking.

"Oh well," my mom said. "Hopefully that never happens."

I nodded, and soon we hung up. But her comment has stayed with me. My mother is working alone in Mankato while my father finishes his final year in St. Croix. I imagine her going through another surgery like the one she had two years ago. What would have happened if her skin cancer had spread? If they hadn't caught it in time? I imagine her getting the news from the doctors as she sat alone in that house, alone like my father. Alone, even, like my grandparents in Missouri. In a recent e-mail, my grandma told me she keeps herself busy around the holidays so that she doesn't get depressed. Her distance from everyone, in so many ways, is why I return to these images of the resort.

And aren't I the same? I hate when Kevin works late and it's just me in the apartment. I hate thinking about my mother and father feeling alone—meandering through empty rooms, slouched in front of televisions and computer screens, as if the flicker could make the time pass. There's comfort in having others around, a physical presence even if you don't actually interact.

When I was in elementary school, I feared the darkness of my bedroom at night. The walls would shudder, fall away into a vacuum, and suddenly there I would be: eons of damp, empty space on all sides, with me suspended in the middle. Utter isolation. A place even God couldn't reach.

In some ways, I've taken it upon myself to ease that sort of isolation in others. I e-mail my grandma, knowing that I'm reaching out to her aloneness. I call my mother on Sunday afternoons just to ask about her week. I Skype with long-distance friends so that they know I am thinking of them—and so that I feel connected.

Yet when I think of what could go wrong here in Binghamton, I come back to aloneness. Kevin hits black ice on the highway during his drive home from work or dies in the night of a diabetic coma, and like my grandmother and mother before me, I am here in this apartment, alone with my grief.

E-MAIL FROM LORI

THAT YEAR, FROM my desk in Binghamton, I e-mail my aunt Lori and ask her to tell me about Sawbill. She replies by attaching a three-page, single-spaced Word document titled "Sawbill for Jennie."

"You want to know about Sawbill," reads the opening line.

After high school, Lori attended the University of Wyoming. My father remembers driving west on I-80 during the holidays to pick her up and then east to take her back. He used to drive it all in one stretch, speeding behind semis, who would motion for him to slow down when their radar picked up a police car.

Lori moved to Montana after Wyoming and has lived on ranches in the country ever since. My family visited when I was in first grade in order to attend one of her weddings. I remember hiking up the mountain in Helena, with the giant, whitewashed cement "H" overlooking the city. We have photographs from the hike—my brother and I near my father, my mother near Lori, who holds my sleeping, toddler sister. Shortly before or shortly after, Lori slept one night on our couch in Minnesota after a late arrival from the airport. My parents had warned me of her presence, but I remember being startled by the blonde hair on the couch pillow, the mass warming the air.

In my grandparents' photo albums, Lori and my father sit side by side on the couch, their legs crossed, their cut-off jean shorts and white T-shirts making them look like twins. In person, Lori is surprisingly loud for someone from that side of the Case family. She jokes with my father, who laughs along with her. She tells family stories at the dinner table. She brings my grandmother bottles of wine to cook with, since none of the stores in Utah sell it.

Out of my dad's three siblings, she and Mark were the first to leave Minnesota. I wanted to believe their leaving made them anomalies.

"If things had been different, I don't know that I would have ever left Sawbill," Lori writes in the second paragraph.

Lori calls herself a country girl. "That tells you I am not a city girl," she writes. "In places like these, without the distractions or the sensory overload in cities, your own senses have control over whether you should be fearful or not. I trust my senses, for better or worse, I trust them.

"Sawbill had it all, the lakes, animals, trees, berries, family, quietness, and beauty. I am pretty sure that your dad took you up there before, so you know what I mean about the beauty. I am sorry you didn't get to enjoy Sawbill the way we did."

Unlike my father, whose answers to my questions have so far been vague, as if he doesn't care or doesn't want to remember, Lori provides specific details. She lists the names of the eleven cabins: Towner, Brookside, Pine Ridge, White Spruce, Pulpwood, Moose, Black Bear, Porcupine, Deer, Otter, and Beaver. She recalls the walk-in fridge beneath the kitchen where she and my father would sneak Tab, Bubble Up, RC Cola, and root beer. She recalls the animal mounts, birch paper lampshades, and wood knot creations that decorated the main rooms of the lodge. She says that the smell of polished wood, pine trees, cedar trees, and fresh-cut pine always takes her mind to Sawbill.

Sawbill was a place of firsts. I was there the first time I fired a gun, waited on tables, first job, first attempt at independence (mom was too busy to watch us all the time), my first canoe, first time cross-country skiing, first time to swim in a lake without supervision, first time cleaning a fish (and many, many, more), first time sneaking through the woods at night, first time up close to a bear, first time driving a truck, and more firsts, but I do not wish to ramble on and bore you.

She says Sawbill was a lot of work, with cleaning cabins, waiting tables, helping in the kitchen, going to the dump, cleaning fish, guiding fishermen, and helping whomever. But it was also a lot of fun. She, Mark, and my father swam, went out in boats, picked blueberries, shot rifles, played what they called "Sawbill poker" with guests, rode a bike with no chains and, one summer, a small motorcycle. My father, she says, rode the chainless bike straight into the lake.

"If things had been different, I don't know that I would have ever left Sawbill," Lori writes.

If things had been different. I do not know what she means by this. If my grandparents had been able to hang on to the resort? If the back taxes and repairs didn't threaten their livelihood? If my grandfather hadn't moved to London for his job with Honeywell? If my grandma and Mary Alice and the outfitters had gotten along?

I imagine some dark undertone, pushing my aunt and my family out of the resort. Some secret, some deep wrong, just under the soil, that my father evades and that Lori buries beneath tales of adolescent independence and joy.

One day, Prince and I were at the dock sitting on the very edge watching the ducks when he started to growl. I turned around to see what he was growling at and there was a bear ambling toward the dock area. I grabbed Prince's collar so he couldn't run. I kept thinking, if it steps on the dock I am jumping in. Too late, I jumped in anyway, dragging Prince with me; we swam across to the peninsula and got out.

Mom was never crazy about the animals. She is a city girl through and through. One summer, we caught some baby ducks and put them in Mom's tub in the Lodge. You should have heard her scream. She was mad at us. They sure were cute.

All of the animals made life so much more enjoyable, just being able to watch them showed you what a great gift this life is.

During my grandparents' stint at Sawbill, my aunt was in elementary school and then middle school—largely the same age as me when my family visited the Superior Hiking Trail most often. In Sawbill, she found an independence she did not have in the Twin Cities. People weren't always watching her. She could try out new hobbies, take pictures of bears to show to her city friends. Sawbill gave her something to brag about, just as backpacking gave me something to brag about at my own Twin Cities middle school. If things had been different . . .

I know that it seems like I am only telling you the good that was Sawbill, and I am. I know we had rough times there (not very many), I just prefer to remember the joy that Sawbill brought to me. I was never afraid for my person while at

Sawbill, even with all the different people that stayed there or at the campgrounds. I was never afraid for me.

I pause here. The truth is, I want the bad times. I want the undertones, the secrets, the grievances that sent my family from that place.

Though maybe, I begin to wonder, there isn't anything that dramatic about why we left. Maybe it was smaller. Maybe Lori never sensed tension between Mary Alice and my grandma. Maybe there wasn't tension. Maybe it is just me, trying to find some dramatic arc that would validate my desire to hang on to these stories, to ask these questions.

If things had been different, my family would have stayed. Lori would have stayed in northern Minnesota, and we'd all still go up there on the holidays to play on the frozen lake and carve chunks of sand out from the frozen waves. I would have learned to shoot a shotgun in those woods. I would have taken a picture of a bear to show my middle school and high school friends. I probably wouldn't have ridden a chainless bike into a lake or gotten on a motorcycle, but I would have canoed by myself. I would have cleaned cabins and helped my grandmother in the kitchen and learned how to skin a fish.

It wouldn't matter that my father left for a job in the Virgin Islands and that my mother joined him. They would return in the summers to help at the resort—or at least to visit for a few weeks, for a month. It wouldn't matter that Kevin and I moved to New York. We, too, would come back for family reunions.

If things had been different, my grandparents would not have moved to Utah and then to four different homes in Missouri. My grandmother would not keep trying to send me her quilts.

When I was in middle school, I considered the North Shore the most beautiful place on earth. I infused it with a spirituality that turned Lake Superior, which we saw from overlooks on the Superior Hiking Trail, into a god. After a day's hike, I'd take my journal back to the nearest overlook, where I'd sit on the red rock cliffs, my feet dangling, Lake Superior glinting on the far horizon like a sliver of metal, the trees beneath me shifting like waves in the breeze. "There's always an overlook. Even after the most difficult climb," I observed.

Lori writes that winter made Sawbill "absolutely the most beautiful, peaceful, and serene place ever"; "I swear if you were there right after a snowstorm or during one, you would know that it was the place people tried to capture in paintings of what winter should look like. The trees would arch over the roads with the wet snow holding them in place. It was magical."

I don't know if this is the kind of information you want.
Hope this helps you.
I hope all is going wonderfully for you.
Aunt Lori.

The simplicity of her ending unsettles me. I am no longer that middle school girl on overlooks, my legs dangling over a rock as I journal about the beauty I see around me. Though I am still apt to find quiet places to sit and journal, to admire the landscape, I don't call things beautiful very often. I haven't felt that at home for a long time.

I am no longer that middle school girl, but after reading Lori's account, I wish I were.

GARDENING WITH RUTH

🌸 ALL SPRING, OUR neighbor Ruth works outside with her hoe, digging up grass to make room for plants. "There she is again," I tell Kevin when I spot her near the fence line, hoe in hand. Though we've lived above her for seven months, ever since we moved to upstate New York from the Midwest, her sudden gardening surprises me. Mornings and nights she works in sweat pants, a handkerchief tied around her head. She bends forward at the hip so that her sweat shirt rides up, revealing slivers of her wide, brown back. She reminds me of a hinge, as if she only has a single joint in her body. The hoe lifts and falls and lifts and falls as she rips sod from the back of the yard near the fence posts or expands semicircles for ferns in the front. She pauses, wipes her forehead, lifts the hoe again.

We saw little of Ruth all winter. A seventy-year-old immigrant from Zimbabwe, she hated the cold. Aside from walks to the bus stop, where she caught a ride to her job at the YWCA daycare, or walks to the brick Methodist church on Main Street, she seemed to spend the winter on her couch, next to the gas fireplace she occasionally asked us to relight. Her daughter, our landlord, thanked us for keeping an eye on her and helping out around the house. But the winter had been long, and I'd worried about Ruth. It relieves me to see her outside.

I pull on a coat and join her. In the dusk, Ruth's breath is heavy. Her teeth shine when I say hello. "Jennie!" she says. "I'm digging up grass! We don't want grass. When I'm done, the entire yard will be a garden. We won't have to mow!" She laughs and shakes her finger at me.

"Need help?" I ask.

"Tonight, no. I'm taking a break. But later, yes. There will be lots of weeding." She wipes her forehead with the back of her hand, puts the hoe in the shed and says good night. I pick up the clumps of dirt she'd broken into and crumble them in my hands. Moist with clay, the dirt stains my fingertips. The dirt is not like the dirt I'd known in Minnesota and Nebraska. Not like the dirt I'd worked the summer before at my grandmother's assisted living unit in Missouri—the small planters in the front yard, the heat beating down. I press the clumps of dirt with my foot and wipe my hands on the grass.

That week Ruth digs up sod in a perimeter along the driveway. She digs up the entire stretch between the sidewalk and street. Each day when I return from work, a little more of the grass is gone. Patches of once-wet earth dry in the sun, clumps of extracted sod stacked like bricks along the perimeter.

In early March, I sign up on a whim for a seed-starting workshop. The workshop, scheduled for the Saturday of Binghamton's St. Patrick's Day Parade, takes place at an urban farm's greenhouse. Since the city has closed off much of Main Street, I walk through downtown, with its mix of early twentieth-century architecture and boarded up storefronts. Parents pull their face-painted children along the sidewalks. Drunk college students stand in clumps near the bar entrances, occasionally falling into me as I push through with my elbows. I weave through the crowds while cars blast their horns on the side streets. Past the YWCA where Ruth works, the houses and apartment complexes slump in disrepair, but at least the crowds lessen. I jump over puddles where the sidewalk has crumbled until I finally make it to the urban farm.

The inside of the greenhouse billows with summer. Condensation runs down the inside of the plastic as fifteen attendees and I pull off our coats. We spend the afternoon poking holes in the bottoms of old yogurt cups that we then fill with peat moss. Once everyone has prepared a handful of yogurt cups, the workshop leader passes out tomato and basil seedlings the size of my pinky. The green seems to glow. I push dirt around the white roots and wonder at the thin capillaries. I could crush them so easily. I smile at the sunlight filtering through the plastic, at the way the wind makes the sides of the greenhouse swell and snap. I've had a garden in nearly every place I've lived, and I realize now that I've missed it. As the workshop leader talks about grow lights, I sprinkle dirt over lettuce seeds and begin to brainstorm vegetables to plant.

By the time the workshop ends, the parade is done. I carry my yogurt containers in a small box, hold the flaps up so that the wind won't shock the plants. My legs grow tired. My hip aches from the afternoon of standing in the greenhouse. Cars speed past and intoxicated teenagers gather in loud groups on front porches and driveways. "What's in the box?" they yell. I walk carefully, the green like a small light in my hands.

A neighbor drops off knots of hostas she's dug up from her own garden. The plants lean against the back shed, their roots like closed fists, the thick leaves starting to droop in the sun. "Look at them! So beautiful!" Ruth says when she returns home. "Do you know who did this?"

I shake my head. Ruth seems to know everyone, and they are always dropping off plants—perennials for the back, strawberries for the small plot near the shed. She'd moved from apartment to apartment for years, until her daughter in California bought this house last spring. Now, all her old neighbors want to help her start her garden.

Ruth and I separate the hostas by cutting through the roots with a knife. I move the clumps from one side of the yard to the other as she decides where to place them. In Zimbabwe, Ruth says, no one had pots. They'd use whatever they could find—garbage bags, cans, buckets with broken bottoms. Ruth stores the previous year's black leaf bags in the shed. She digs them out, fills them with leaves and dirt. We plant a few hostas inside each, lean them against the side of the house. I wonder what will happen in the winter—if the frost and snow will shred the bottoms and cause the dirt to spill from split sides. But Ruth is proud. "See," she tells me. "Perfect. People here throw away too much."

When we finish, we wipe our hands on our pant legs and sit on the front porch. Kids yell from the park behind the house. A neighbor waves at Ruth while walking past with her dogs. "This is Jennie, she lives upstairs," Ruth says, nodding toward me. The neighbor smiles and moves on.

"How is New York?" Ruth asks. "How is everything upstairs?"

"Good," I say. "We're still getting settled, but we like New York so far." I do not tell her how strapped we are for money. How, lately, I've found myself wondering if moving here was the right choice. Most of the people I know leave Binghamton during the summer, but Kevin and I have to stay. The thought depresses me. I sigh and turn to Ruth. "When did you first come to New York?" I ask.

Ruth folds her hands over her stomach and leans back. "In the 1970s," she says. When they arrived, the relative they'd arranged to pick them up went to the wrong airport. Or the plane had to land at a different airport. Or they just got confused. Either way, Ruth says, they were stuck at JFK, with no money and no place to go until they could get ahold of their relatives. They had three young children, all hungry and tired. "We sat at the food court," Ruth tells me. "But we had no money. No money at all." They stared at the vendors, at the other passengers buying burgers and french fries. Their stomachs rumbled; the children began to cry and whine. Ruth says she was still breastfeeding her youngest. After two hours, Ruth's husband approached one of the vendors, explained the situation, and asked if he could give them some french fries.

"And he did!" Ruth says. After the dinner rush, when the food court was starting to close down and the vendors had extra burgers and fries, they gave them some more. "We said we'd pay them once my aunt arrived, but they said no problem. No problem. Everyone here was an immigrant once." She shakes her head, smiles. "People told us New Yorkers were mean. People say that today, too. But they were not mean to us."

"That's great," I say. "That a really great story."

"Um hm." Ruth beams.

"People in the Midwest also think New Yorkers are mean," I say. I think about the last time I saw my grandmother, how she'd insisted I take pepper spray with me. "Here, take this," she'd said, forcing the small black case into my luggage.

I do not want to infringe on Ruth's garden, so I sign up for a community garden plot a few blocks away from the apartment building. Before the last frost, I carry a notebook and a pencil to the garden. I draw the plot, stand in front of it as I think about my design—where I want the rows of carrots, onions, and peas. Someone has planted strawberries, and the new growth already peaks through last year's compost. Spiky green leaves emerge from the earth, covering a third of the raised bed. I transplant a few strawberry shoots to another community bed on the side of the yard. Teenagers yell to each other as they pass along the sidewalk, on the way to the Wendy's or McDonald's near Main Street. Steam lifts from the dry cleaners next door. In the distance, basketballs thud on the concrete of the park. As I work, the shadow of the house next door moves toward me, until the tip of its roof pokes into the southeast corner of the plot. But still I keep working. I work until my fingers grow cold. Until dirt stains the creases of my knuckles.

I used to help my grandmother garden. I can imagine planting something in nearly every yard she's lived in—marigolds around the lake home in northern Minnesota, beans in the vegetable plot of the ranch home near the river. When she moved to Utah, we drove to the nursery and marveled at all the new species we could choose from. We decided on three oleanders, which we planted near the orange tree in the tiny backyard. She had a crab apple tree at the first house in Missouri, hens and chicks along the rocky patio of the second. This summer, she and Grandpa have moved again, and I wonder what she's growing, if anything. She writes that she's depressed. They live too far away to visit family. "Maybe we can come by next year," my grandma says, but it's unlikely. Grandpa can't see enough to drive. He can no longer feel his fingers.

My grandmother's sadness runs down my throat. She has lived in so many places—has had to set down roots so many times. When I get back from the community garden, I look at pictures of her in Minnesota, Iowa, Missouri, Utah. I taste the dust from Utah when we walked to the swimming pool, the sharp gullies along the rural roads in Missouri. The apples from the bluffs in southeast Minnesota, the fish from northern lakes.

I go back even further—to her honeymoon in Kentucky where Grandpa was stationed and the two years in England, where my grandmother developed a love of tea and scones. I taste it all, but still, when I close my eyes, I see her crying at the end of driveways—driveways from every city she has moved to and every city I've left.

Ruth's daughter and son-in-law arrive in early May to make raised beds for a vegetable garden. They fly in from California and rent a car, which they use to transport 2 x 8-inch planks of wood from the lumberyard. For two days, the son-in-law and daughter measure the yard and cut the lumber with a small jigsaw borrowed from a friend. They thread an extension cord through the basement and use a drill to build the beds. Ruth walks out from the kitchen, stands with her hands on her hips, nods and smiles. They fill the raised beds with last year's leaves and bring in a truckload of topsoil. Ruth drags a plastic chair from the back porch and spends the next few evenings planting seeds and moving seedlings from one plot to another. When neighbors stop to admire the garden, she beams. Her high voice carries to our upstairs apartment.

When the raised beds are full, Ruth plants sunflowers between the sidewalk and street. She also plants sweet potatoes and squash, marigolds to keep the rabbits away. She pokes at weeds with a metal prong and waters the ground until the sidewalks gleam from runoff. On weekends, I help her weed until my back aches. "Thank you, thank you," she says. "It looks beautiful. So beautiful."

One day Ruth calls, her voice quavering. I can't make out the words on my cell phone and tell her I'll come down.

When I meet her in the backyard, her face is drawn, her forehead furrowed.

"Someone has gotten in," she says.

"To your apartment?" I ask.

"No, to the backyard. Someone has broken through the fence."

She leads me behind the shed, where a thin sheet of chicken

wire connects a gap in the chain-link fence. The chicken wire is distended and limp, as if someone, or something, had fallen on it.

"Maybe it's a dog," I say. Every evening around seven, the woman next door throws a tennis ball to her collie for half an hour. If the tennis ball took an odd bounce, the dog certainly might have bent the fence.

"No," Ruth says. "A dog couldn't do this." She shakes her head, scans the large city park that shares a border with the backyards of all the homes on our side of the street. On warm days, teenagers breakdance in the park's gazebo. Older adults sometimes smoke marijuana on the benches. "It was a person," Ruth says. "Someone got in."

"Are you sure? I really think a dog might have done it."

"No," Ruth insists. "It was a person."

We scan the inside of the shed, but nothing is missing. The door to the basement is locked.

"Someone got in," Ruth keeps saying. "I thought you should know someone got in."

I frown, stare at the bent bit of fence. "That's horrible," I say. "But they didn't take anything. It looks like whatever it was just passed through."

"Uh uh uh," she says. "This is not right. Not right at all." Ruth shakes her head and walks back into her apartment.

That evening, I tell Kevin about the conversation. Once, Ruth asked us to carry an old wooden ladder into the basement. She'd found it along the curb and dragged it behind the shed, where the metal had rusted. We didn't think the ladder was worth saving, and it was too big to maneuver into the main section of the basement, but we did as she asked, tying the ladder to the basement railing with old extension cords. "Ruth thought someone would steal that ladder, and now she's worried about the fence," I whisper. "She's just anxious," I conclude.

But the next morning, I find an empty beer bottle stuffed beneath the chain link fence. The day after that, a crumbled McDonald's bag, spotted with grease. I start to think a person, might, indeed, have bent the fence, perhaps when running from the cops. It was a big dent. Too big for a dog.

Two days later, Ruth calls out to me from behind the screen of her front door. I can barely make out her silhouette from the darkness of the room. "Sorry for bothering you about the fence," she says. "I get so nervous. Because of the war." She pauses, tightens her hand against the side of the door she's holding open. "Bad things happened. In Zimbabwe. The war was a long time ago. My daughter says I'm silly, but I panic. I get nervous. I'm not the same." She pulls at the bottom of her sweatshirt. Her eyes glint in the dark.

"It's okay," I say. "Don't worry about it. And it did look like something got through and bent the fence. I would have been nervous, too."

"But it was just a dog," she says. "A dog."

"Yes," I say to the outline of her body in the doorframe. "I'm sure it was a dog."

Sometimes I wonder if Ruth gardens for the same reasons I do—the way it makes me feel part of the landscape, the place. I spend evenings and weekends tilling the soil, planting my rows, watching for weeds, and in doing so reminding myself of what I'd always known: how much I need the practice of gardening to care about my new community. I need the rhythm of it all—the almost daily weeding, the evening trips to the garden to cut lettuce for dinner or collect a handful of strawberries from the communal patch. As I run my hands over the onion leaves, feel the weight of the growing tomatoes, and pick squash bug eggs from the undersides of zucchini leaves, I once again, in a quiet way, begin to feel like a participant in this particular ecosystem—a fellow species entangled in it all.

Yet Ruth's displacement is so much more complicated than mine. She lives alone, her children across the city, the state, the country. Her husband is back in Zimbabwe, whether because he wants to be or has to be, I do not know. Ruth doesn't think she will see him again. Some nights, we hear Ruth's voice bubble and echo through the floorboards. The vowels are strange to us—round and cheeky. She speaks loudly, as if through a bad connection, and I imagine her raising her voice to the cell phone, to the computer screen.

Her apartment is full of used furniture and old afghans. When we moved in and couldn't fit Kevin's desk up the stairs, she bought it from us, even though she already had one. She told us her daughter could use it when she visited from California. Family photographs fill the walls. Sunlight glows through closed drapes—so different from our own green and blue walls, our carefully placed furniture, the dining room table and its almost matching brown chairs. Ruth dragged the neighbors' chewed up patio table to our backyard when they were evicted. She found a tan reclining chair by the side of the road and set it on the front porch. When Kevin wants to buy another bookcase, I say we don't have room—for everything that comes in, something must go out—as if we have the privilege to discard things, to have enough.

When Ruth's strawberries refuse to flower due to lack of sun, I cut a handful from my own small patch. She accepts the strawberries with cupped palms and pops one into her mouth, stem and all. "So sweet!" she tells me, her lips pursed, her forehead lifted to the sun.

I e-mail my grandmother photographs of the garden. I tell her how high the tomato plants have grown. I write about the eggplant someone stole just as it ripened, about Ruth's sunflower seeds, sprouting in the front yard. I do not yell into my phone or computer at night, but sometimes it feels like it as I type out my messages, attach my photographs. My grandma in Missouri, I in New York, all that distance between us.

The sunflowers next to the road grow taller than Ruth predicted. Five feet, then six feet, then eight feet. Thick stalks that hardly bend in the wind. They look like trees and are impossible to miss. I keep expecting the city to order us to chop them down.

Ruth is embarrassed. "I didn't know they would get that big!" she insists. She asks me to take a photograph with my digital camera so that she can show her daughter in California. "I thought three feet, four feet," she says, gesturing near her stomach with a flat hand. "Not this! They haven't even bloomed."

"Well, gardening is all an experiment, right?" I say.

Ruth laughs, a long, loud laugh that makes the leaves in the trees ripple. "Yes. And next year, I'm planting these sunflowers in the back!"

I smile and wave as I walk to the community garden. I pull the weeds, check for bugs, and pick the produce that's ready. When I return, Ruth is still in the front, shaking her head at the sunflowers.

"Look what I harvested," I say, showing her a bucketful of snap peas and carrots.

"So beautiful," Ruth tells me.

"You can have some," I say. "Here." I empty a handful into her open hands.

She picks a snap pea from her palm and it crunches between her front teeth.

"Wonderful!" she tells me. "So sweet." She closes her eyes, smiles so that I can see her gums. "This will be dinner. Here. Come." Ruth walks toward the raised beds. She reaches into the plot she'd been weeding earlier that day, twists a green pepper from a plant.

"Here," she says. "And take some zucchini too. I can't eat it all."

I wonder if my grandmother is happy at her new place in Missouri. I wonder if anyone watches out for her—helps her garden and weed. I wonder if Ruth is happy here. Or if she still misses Zimbabwe after all these years. Maybe such longings fade with time, made lighter by the routines of gardening and work. I pluck a zucchini from its bushy hill. "I think I'll make zucchini bread," I tell Ruth.

"Then you'll need more than one. Here, take more," she says, filling my arms with squash.

RESEARCH

🌼 THE SUMMER OF 2011, I work as the content editor of the graduate school's website. I catch the bus to campus before Kevin awakes and spend nine hours in a frigid, air-conditioned office. Kevin and I had planned to explore upstate New York this summer, but our schedules do not align. We only have Sundays together and cannot travel far. I trudge through the park to the bus stop in the morning and trudge home in the afternoon. When my alarm goes off each day, I slap at the button and frown.

It's a loneliness, a lack of satisfaction, that makes me suddenly eye pregnant women. After a year and a half of marriage, the possibility of starting a family opens itself like the zucchini blossoms in my garden. At the office, I slow while working on the pages for graduate student parents. I research daycare options and read about parent-infant swimming lessons at the campus pool. I study our health insurance's maternity benefits. Each day at four o'clock, I watch an increasingly pregnant woman make her way from another office to her car. Soon that could be me. I am finishing my first comprehensive exam at the end of the summer and plan to take the last two by this time next year. At that point, I'll only have my dissertation left: the qualification Kevin and I had created when discussing when to have children. In fact, we could technically start trying within the next six months. The thought both pleases and surprises me.

As the afternoon sun glares through the windows and the computer screen flickers, I count forward and backwards in nine-month intervals. I make a timeline for the rest of my degree, mapping out summer jobs and comp exams—everything I need to do to graduate on time and still start a family.

I begin to see young families everywhere. At a summer parade, parents hold babies while toddlers and young children wobble or sprint for candy. A pregnant woman and her husband lay down in the shade of a tree. She moves from one side to another, pushing herself up when she gets uncomfortable. She closes her eyes and smiles into the sun. Yes, I think: we could start a family here. Here, in this city where we have health insurance that covers maternity stays in both major hospitals, as well as care at the OBGYN clinic less than a mile from our home. Here, in this apartment by the park, where couples both older and younger than us already push strollers. Why not? As June moves into July, and July into August, Kevin and I discuss our options over dinner on our back porch.

"We have decent health insurance. We'll be here for three more years anyway," I say. "It would be better to start a family now than closer to my graduation. Who knows where we'll be then."

Kevin reaches for my hand as Binghamton transforms into something more real to us: its rolling foothills and flooded rivers, its decaying buildings and tree-lined streets. It's not just a place to pass through or a place to stay for these four years but something softer on the edges. Something more lasting and somehow permanent.

That winter, I complete my comprehensive exams and buy prenatal vitamins, which I hide in the closet when family visits for

Thanksgiving. I'm not yet ready to discuss possibilities or to answer questions about "when." The sky lowers itself, a gray fog that will last until spring, and in the warmth of our apartment, with casseroles and bread in the oven, I start rereading the Sawbill book. It causes me to dwell so much on my family's history that I wake early and cannot fall back asleep. I curl on my bed, one hand beneath my pillow, and stare into the closet, where shirts on hangers form a dark curtain.

In my mind, the various storylines intertwine to form a knot of longing and dislocation:

The original owners of Sawbill came from Chicago. None of them grew up along the North Shore.

Shortly after my grandparents gave up the resort in the 1970s, the forest service bought the land, adding it to the Boundary Waters Canoe Area where Kevin and I got engaged.

In fact, the forest service bought Sawbill Resort in 1982, around the same time my grandma joined my grandfather in England—a displacement that has haunted me just as much as Sawbill itself.

When I first saw my dad's copy of the Sawbill book—the book that launched this long obsession—I was digging for the Boundary Waters map that hangs on our wall in Binghamton.

I push myself out of bed and make a pot of coffee. I read and sort through pictures, and the knowledge I gain is gratifying. From a blurry figure in my memory, Sawbill emerges as an actual location with log walls and well-trod paths between cabins. It has a history worthy of a two hundred-plus-page local history book and an archive at the Cook County Historical Museum.

In the 1930s, the Civilian Conservation Corps (CCC) once had a camp there. The small track of land, sloping down to Sawbill Lake, played a role in the outdoor recreation and conservation movements that led to the establishment of the Boundary Waters.

Sawbill has been molded by larger cultural and geological

movements. Like the anorthosite knobs of the Sawtooth mountains—thrust from the earth's crust and then worn down—or the deep gouging of Lake Superior's base, carved from glaciers as they moved south and then north, Sawbill has been pressed, shaped, formed, coiled. The imprints of larger forces still show themselves on the dirt of its trails, the paper pages of its history.

This is a place worthy of attention.

Yet my research also subdues me. As the context grows, my own place in the story diminishes.

I become smaller and smaller and smaller, pushed out of the narrative by the black and white photographs of CCC men in button-up shirts and muddy boots, by the postcards the Argobusts hand-addressed to Chicago businessmen, advertising the opening of a new resort where "folks" canoe into "deep almost unknown forests" and "fish in lakes which seldom have been fished by anyone save Indians."

I lose grasp of the original memories that link me to the area, and the history takes over until I'm not sure what I have left: just nostalgia? Sentiment?

Or, perhaps more perplexing—merely a fiction. For, as I research, I make the place meaningful to me in new ways, drawing connections that I didn't know of before. It is a cognitive act. The small girl with mud on her socks slinks behind the alder, slips behind a strand of birch, to make room for the graduate researcher: the baby-conscious newlywed who surrounds herself with papers and photographs, claiming what perhaps she should not claim.

There on the office floor, with my quilting supplies in the closet and jazz music coming from the radio in the other room, I link my experience at the Sawbill parking lot to the Argobusts' initial arrival. I link those four years that my father summered at Sawbill to the Sentys' decision to sell it in 1982. In my trip to Brule Lake with Kevin, I see myself stepping on the same ground as those

CCC men, touching the same water as Jean Raiken had decades before.

I link my experiences to the experiences of all involved in the lodge and I say, "This is so. This is the way it is."

As if I am elbowing my way in. With a pen in one hand and my black notebook in the other, I push past Jean Raiken and Wilson Argobust and Mary Alice Hansen and the entire Civilian Conservation Corps and the US Forest Service. I say, "Don't forget about me. I belong here too." And as I stand there, between these slightly perplexed figures with their labeled archival folders and their smug authority, I both applaud myself for my bravery, my bravado, and then berate myself for being so rude.

APPALACHIAN TRAIL

 IN JUNE 2011, Kevin and I drive down to the Delaware Water Gap to hike with my brother. We meet in a small gravel parking lot off of the interstate—a parking lot already thick with cars from New Jersey and New York. The interstate murmurs behind us, and cars continue to stream in, circling the gravel lot again and again for a spot. After consulting the trail postings and the paper maps we'd printed out that morning, we decide on a 7.5-mile loop to Sunfish Pond.

"Ready?" I say. "This should be fun."

My brother nods as Kevin adjusts his baseball cap. We pack our lunch in a backpack and fill our water bottles from the spouts near the start of the trail. It is sixty degrees—a beautiful day. I hadn't at first been sure of the trip; though we'd all admired the Water Gap from the interstate—its thousand-foot valley, its water-falls and cliffs—the two-hour drive to meet my brother, followed by the hike and the two-hour drive back had unnerved me. I didn't know what the trail would be like, or if our car, which accu-mulated most of its hundred thousand miles on flat Midwestern highways and didn't particularly enjoy these mountains and hills, would even make it there. When I woke up that morning and had a cup of coffee, my heartbeat had quickened from a combination of caffeine and nerves.

But as we begin the trail, maneuvering around boulders and meandering along the stream, I start to relax. We discuss school and the summer in soft tones. My brother will attend a mathematics conference in Europe this summer, I am working my summer office job, and Kevin has just started a new position at a museum. Our brief updates and questions about work and school settle onto the path like last year's leaves, and soon we are quiet, each of us breathing slow, steady breaths. Couples with backpacking gear and bandanas tied around their foreheads pass us as they head back to the parking lot. Not too long ago, that would have been my family. That would have been us.

The trail begins to climb so that sometimes the boulders form a stairway. We ascend, stopping every now and then to rest, to look at the trees that sway in the breeze, to follow our location on the small paper map. My back grows sweaty, but the breeze is cool. It feels refreshing to be outside, to be moving. It feels like something I'm good at, something I've done before.

After another mile or so, we spot a fork in the road. Here the trees spread out, though the ground stays damp, leaves and pine needles like a thick carpet between them. Larger boulders emerge from the earth—boulders big enough to climb or sit on if you wanted to try. If we were still children, my brother and I would do just that, like we did on all the boulders along Lake Superior's North Shore. We'd stick our feet into nooks and crannies, pull ourselves up by gripping small crevices. A handful of photographs from that time show us on the tops of large, red rocks, gazing at rain puddles teaming with larvae. Fluorescent bandanas frame our faces. Oversized sunglasses slip from our noses. We'd squat there for what seemed like hours until my parents called us away. Then, my brother would leap down, landing with a spray of pebbles. I'd sit on the top of the rock and slide off more slowly, one hand guiding me down, the other outstretched.

Now we pass the rocks without stopping. We move through the trees, following the thin path toward the lake. The breeze strengthens up here, whipping the brush that borders the path. Through gaps in the trees, the foothills of Pennsylvania and the Poconos roll below us. Soon, the mountaintop lake emerges, the water a glassy stillness among the green. Small groups of hikers stake out picnic tables and fallen logs for lunch. We walk a ways around the lake until we, too, find a fallen log. We open the backpack, take out our package of tortillas and the jars of peanut butter and honey. We smear the peanut butter on thick, drizzle it with honey, and then either roll the tortilla or fold it like a taco, washing the hefty lunch down with water, with apples, with trail mix we've bagged for the afternoon. It tastes like all the tortilla sandwiches I've eaten when camping—the thick feeling at the back of my throat, the film of peanut butter and flour on my tongue.

Black flies and mosquitoes buzz around our heads. We swat at them and adjust our caps, as if we've always been up here, in this area, eating tortillas, swatting at bugs, and maneuvering around boulders. As if we are comfortable here, the area familiar, the log we straddle a log we have sat on before.

After lunch clouds roll in, filling the forest with chilled shadows. We hike back to the parking lot, where I pull out a Tupperware container of rhubarb muffins I'd made the day before. We sit on tree roots at the edge of the trailhead and eat the muffins, licking our fingers free of the sticky residue. "This was fun. We should do it again," I say.

"Yes, we should," my brother, Jeff, answers.

I snap the lid on the now empty Tupperware. We stand and cross our arms beneath the trees. More cars enter the parking lot, searching for a spot. A few young boys fish in the stream.

"I suppose we should start back. It's a bit of a drive," Jeff says.

"Yes, I suppose."

We stand there a minute or two longer, looking at the path we've just hiked. Darker clouds begin to move in.

"I guess," I say. But before we leave, I take a photograph of the Appalachian Trail sign that marked the start of our hike. Brown with white lettering and scratched in places, the sign slants on its pole, as if someone swung something at it or kicked it with a steel-toed boot. Foliage fills the background of the photograph with a deep, unwavering green.

I text the photograph to my father in the Virgin Islands. "Guess where we are?" I write.

Within a few minutes, my phone buzzes with his reply. "I wish I could have joined you!" the text says.

I hold the phone in my hand, gaze at the dark pixels forming his message, and shiver, slightly, in the wind. I wish he could have joined us, too. I slip my phone into my pocket like a smooth stone, but as Kevin turns west onto I-80 and my brother turns east, a heaviness settles into my toes. My dad always wanted to hike that trail. After our family had backpacked most of the Superior Hiking Trail, he began purchasing books about the Appalachian Trail—nonfiction readers like Bill Bryson's *A Walk in the Woods* as well as how-to guides with detailed descriptions of topography and reviews of campsites.

"Your metabolism reaches peak capacity after just a few weeks," he told me one night at the dinner table. "Ready to join me?"

I was in high school by that time. We'd just moved from the Twin Cities to Mankato, and I was still lonely enough to go to coffee shops with my parents whenever they invited me, but embarrassed enough to lower my head whenever I saw someone from school. "How long will it take?" I asked.

"Oh, three, four, maybe five months. We can go the summer after you graduate from high school and return just in time for college. How about that?"

I stared at him, wide-eyed. "All summer?"

"Quite the summer! And you'll start college in the best shape of your life."

"Maybe. I'll think about it," I said, twirling a string of spaghetti, or whatever pasta we were having that night, around my fork.

I thought the topic would blow over, but for more than a year he brought it up. The Appalachian Trail: a hike we'd complete after I finished high school. For the most part, I played along. "Maybe." I'd always say. Or, "Sounds interesting. Yes, that could be fun." But I knew even then that we'd never go—that it was just a dream of his—and that I really didn't want to spend my entire summer before college climbing through damp woods and eating those endless peanut butter and honey tortilla wraps, even if it meant my metabolism neared 100 percent efficiency. I wanted to earn money and hang out with friends. A three-month trip on the Appalachian Trail sounded like an obligation—something I'd trudge through, longing for it to end.

But now, as Kevin and I drive away from my brother, through the Poconos toward Scranton and then north up I-81, I really wish that I had taken that trip with my father. So many of his dreams, it seems, have become just that: dreams. The cabin in northern Minnesota. The excursion to Alaska. The sailing trip from St. Croix to the continental United States.

He will never accomplish all that he once wanted to accomplish—neither will I—and someday he will pass away, leaving a loss larger than Sawbill. Why couldn't I have at least shared his enthusiasm?

His sadness in not being with us today, in not partaking on our small hike, lingers in the cushions of my chair, in the calluses of my feet, lingers as we return to postindustrial Binghamton and our quiet apartment. My father, popping Ibuprofen on our bike rides, relaxing on the Superior Hiking Trail—his love for the trees and the sky and the early morning call of birds as necessary to protect as my own.

RETURN TO MINNESOTA

❦ IN THE SPRING of 2012, I find out that I'm pregnant and that I've earned a grant to conduct research back on the North Shore. The funds will allow me to visit the building that once housed the lodge, now renovated and moved to a new site, as well as the county's local historical society. I am thrilled with both. All winter, as Kevin and I discussed starting a family, I'd thought about returning to the North Shore. I *needed* to, I'd realized, in order to wrap up loose ends and come to terms with my infatuation. After three years in St. Croix, my father had found a new job, and that summer both of my parents would move to Florida. I needed to see the area once more, before children complicated travel and I had no immediate family members left in Minnesota. Like an odd gnawing, an itch on the underside of my foot, I recognized that something had to be done—it wasn't a choice.

Yet when my semester ends and summer finally arrives, I still haven't made travel arrangements.

"When are you coming?" my mom asks when I call her on a Sunday early in May.

"I'm not sure. I have to figure some things out. Probably mid-June. When are you done teaching?"

"The seventh," she says. "Though your dad will be gone through the ninth."

"Oh," I reply. I had been hoping to go early in June, in order to attend a small surprise party my dad and aunt have planned for my grandparents' sixtieth wedding anniversary. But if I visit the North Shore before the anniversary party, my parents won't be able to join me. I pick at my fingernails and stall until I can control my voice. Though I never told my parents that I want them to come along, I realize now how important it is to me.

"Well, let us know," my mom says.

"I will," I tell her. "I just need to figure some things out first." But really I am putting it off, worried the trip won't turn out the way I want it to: no one will join me, and I'll be too tired from the pregnancy to cleanly wrap up of all these loose ends I've been pinching between my fingers.

We talk about school, the end of her year, all the packing before she can put the house on the market. "There's so much work to do. It will never get done, especially with your dad not here," she says. I tell her to hang in there, that in a few months it will all be over, but we end the conversation soon after, and when the phone is silent I find myself thinking of nostalgia.

Is my obsession with Sawbill merely nostalgia? I got married, am now pregnant, and my parents are selling my childhood home. All the tangible holds to my childhood are disappearing; I am leaving it behind and can no longer pretend I am still that young child with the hiking stick, mud caked on my socks. I cannot pretend that we are that same family, with our weeklong trips to the Superior Hiking Trail. Soon, my parents will leave Minnesota, and we may never go back.

I pace the apartment and stare out of the windows. What I want, I realize, is a visible family history. I want a lifetime of gulps before tunnels. I want to tighten my child's backpacking straps. More than anything, I want my grandparents and parents and children to all share a loved place, so that I can sense their footprints in the dirt and pine needles, their breath in the air.

Near the end of May, my mom calls me to tell me that after six days on the market they've sold the house.

"Wow. That's great," I tell her.

"I know," she says, her voice tired, yet relieved. "One thing we don't have to worry about anymore. We still have to get through the inspection, of course, but we've accepted the offer and their loan has gone through."

We talk through the details and the next steps for moving, and then she asks again about my trip to Minnesota. My brother, it turns out, will be in town for a long weekend but not until after my parents drive to Missouri. As my mom lists off dates, I eye the calendar on my desk and the quickly shrinking span of days my family will be in one place. My mom ends the call by saying she's not sure any of them will be able to join me up north but that at least we can all be in Minnesota for a few days.

After we hang up, I take my phone to the back porch that overlooks the park and sit in one of the camping chairs we keep there, next to the small greenhouse, misty with condensation from the lettuce and tomato seedlings I have yet to transplant into the garden.

My parents have sold the house, I tell myself. *My trip in June might be the last time I go back.* I repeat these lines to myself again and again, but still I don't feel anything—not that sudden tightening like a few months ago when my mom first told me that my dad had accepted a job in Florida. After I'd hung up with her last time, I'd chopped vegetables in the kitchen for homemade pizza. Kevin found me there, dicing the onions into finer and finer slivers, my eyes wet and red.

"What's wrong?" he'd asked.

"Nothing," I'd said. "It's just the onions."

"No, it isn't." he replied. "What's wrong?"

But it took him three more tries before I answered his question, the knife rhythmic as a lawnmower on the cutting board.

Now, however, I feel nothing. I breathe in and out, my jaw muscles loose. I squint into the sun, then down at the floor where bits of pollen and dead ants have collected on the rough green carpet.

Would the actual selling of the house have affected me more a year or two ago? When marriage was still so new to me? When Kevin and I felt isolated here in New York? I reimagine those long evenings, when the distance between here and Minnesota stretched thin as a string.

Maybe I'm just tired of thinking about it all. In the park, city workers in orange vests mow the lawn and use weed whackers around the trunks of the oak trees, while cardinals and sparrows jump from branch to branch.

This is the life we have chosen for ourselves, I tell myself. There is no reason to fear a future I cannot surmise, and maybe the idea of a settled past is so foreign to me now—so surreal—that I can't even dream about it. My parents are leaving Minnesota for good. My sister is moving to Buffalo. Next year, my brother will look for a new job. In two years, Kevin and I will as well. Why bother imagining a time when we could have been in one place?

I barrage myself with the facts of our migrations and separations, as if trying to get at some sort of emotion, but I can't. My breathing is even, my feet firm on the ground.

A spider web billows on the clotheslines that run from our porch to one of the trees across the yard. The tops of the oak trees sway. Such emptiness. I stare at the sky, waiting for time to pass— for whatever will happen to happen.

I fly into Minneapolis on a Monday in mid-June. I will join my parents when they visit my grandparents in Missouri. I will then stay two nights at Solbakken Resort, in one of the units built out of the transported Sawbill Lodge, followed by three nights farther north in Grand Marais.

"Don't you look straight out of the northwoods," my mom says of the blue boonie hat Kevin had plopped on my head just as I'd left the apartment in Binghamton. Though the temperature in central Minnesota is in the mid-eighties, I am wearing jeans, a T-shirt, and a fleece jacket in order to save space in my single carry-on and backpack. As my dad opens the trunk, I unzip my fleece, roll it into a ball, and lay it on top of the carry-on my dad has now placed in the car.

I have flown into this airport so many times, it is hard to believe I may not return here again for a while. As we drive the hour and a half southwest to Mankato, we skirt southern Minneapolis, cutting through the business district of Bloomington, with the large signs for the Mall of America and IKEA, for Best Buy's headquarters, the eight-lane highway dotted with hotels and motels and business parks with a few office lights still lit in the night.

Traffic thins once we reach Edina, with its mansions and upscale shopping districts, and then thins even more once we dip into the Minnesota River valley, a shallower river valley than the Mississippi but one that nonetheless has carved bluffs of the farmland. The hills seem smaller after Binghamton's foothills, and I wonder if I'll ever get back here after this summer—if a friend's wedding or a high school reunion will tempt me to drive these roads once more. Somehow I doubt it. Yet the sight of my old neighborhood, the one-and-a-half-story house with the "For Sale" sign in front, makes me sigh and give a half smile. "Familiarity," the word I return to again and again. How much I appreciate the simplicity of objects I recognize.

We leave the next day for Missouri, driving eleven hours to my grandparents' newest living quarters in Springfield. I have told myself that I will interview my family members on the way down, but the timing never feels right. Instead I stare out the windows, do a Sudoku puzzle, and read through old copies of my mother's *Ladies' Home Journal*. My sister and mom read their own books while my dad drives, occasionally rubbing his eyes. He hopes we get there before dark since he doesn't like to drive at night anymore.

When I was younger and we drove through Iowa and Missouri, we always complained about how flat it was. Now, however, I find myself content with the view. More than ten shades of green speckle the grassy fields, while yellow, purple, and white wildflowers spot the sides of the highway. The land rolls up and down in faint waves, as if a boat had passed through at a slow speed a few minutes before. The Midwest is entering its worst drought in years, but this early in the summer, the crops are still growing, the leaves on trees drooping just slightly in the sun.

We pull into Springfield just after dark, and the next day we meet up with my aunt, uncle, and cousin before surprising my grandparents by showing up at their front door. "Look who's here," my grandpa says while my grandma covers her mouth, cries, and then rushes off to take the rollers from her hair. We crowd the living room with the laughter and small talk of a family that doesn't see each other often but genuinely gets along. Next to each other, my aunt Lindy and grandma look like replicas, while my cousin Joel, twenty-one and muscular from weightlifting and his job at the auto body shop, towers above them both. Aside from quick visits during high school graduation open houses, I've hardly seen him since my grandparents moved to Utah nearly a decade ago, even though my aunt Lindy, uncle Lorren, and cousins Josh and Joel have always lived in Minnesota—three to four hours north of us.

In fact, they still live within an hour of each other, Josh now married with a stepdaughter and a recently purchased house. They drive snowmobiles and have fishing licenses and go to the race-tracks on the weekends where the two boys race hobby cars.

In my grandparents' living room, Lindy shows us pictures of both cousins in their cars, their sunglasses slick on their faces. "Josh didn't do too bad until his motor went," she says, her Minnesota accent so much thicker than mine is now, so much thicker than my father's or my mother's, all of us of too mobile, too used to other accents, other voices, to have retained that solid "O," the long "A."

I listen to her describe Josh's blown motor and then to Joel describe his own auto work—the day they had to bring each car back from the racetrack one at a time because the second trailer busted. My own brother is somewhere at a mathematics convention in Taiwan, a notebook open as he writes out long equations in pencil. Such different lives, and who is to say which is better? Which is ideal?

When my uncle asks how things are going in New York, I sputter out some reply about school going well and Kevin enjoying his job, though I also can't help but feel that New York doesn't exist in this room, with the photographs of cars and the glass-topped coffee table. New York is a map none of us have traveled. A place I inhabit but where I don't really belong. And although my uncle's interest pleases me, I want to stuff New York beneath my shirt or back into my suitcase, pretend it is just a temporary trip, a small adventure, and not some symbol for the life Kevin and I will now lead—this thinning of accents, this forgetting how to fish.

"And Jennie, you're going to Grand Marais after this?" my aunt asks. "Joel and I almost went up there a month or so ago, didn't we Joel," she says, glancing at my cousin. My aunt laughs. "I don't remember what happened. I just wanted to go up there and see it—maybe stop by the old resort—but I forgot how long of a drive it was. By the time we got to Two Harbors, we decided to turn back."

"Two Harbors," my dad says. "You were almost there."

"Almost, but not quite," she says.

And again the strangeness of the situation makes me want to lie, to cringe, to pretend I don't need a research grant to get up there, but that, like them, I could just drive out some Sunday. No big deal. No planning. Heritage there to be visited, or ignored, not studied under some sort of pretense requiring proposals and grants.

"Speaking of old homes, we were thinking of getting out to the farm," my aunt says. "It sure would be good to see it one last time. How far is it from here?"

"Oh, I don't know," my grandpa says, slow, a hand on the scrubble of his chin.

"About an hour, hour and a half out," my grandma says, "and then an hour and a half back. So you'll need at least a good three hours."

"What farm?" I ask.

"My brother's," my grandma says. "He's moved in with Karen, so they're selling it." Her lips grow tight. Her brother has lived in Missouri his whole life—one of the reasons she and grandpa moved here after Utah—but now her brother has dementia. I never realized he lived that close—or that he was rooted so long on this land.

"We were thinking of stopping on the way home." My aunt adds. "Joel hasn't seen it, and it's not too far from the farm where Lorren grew up."

"It's been more than twenty years," Lorren says, his voice like the bark of an old tree, falling off in soft chunks.

"Do you remember the old farm in Nevada?" my aunt asks my dad.

"Sure I do," he says.

"We used to go there all the time as kids." My aunt sighs. "It sure would be good to see it again."

I frown. If we have family history in Missouri and Iowa, why is it the North Shore I long for? There are other places I could have attached to: the barn of this farm in Missouri, supposedly, the broad sweep of these ranches, the walnut trees and armadillos.

Of course, I never visited Missouri until Grandma and Grandpa moved there after Utah. My father did not take us here on camping trips. We did not pack up the backpacks and the bear canisters and head south.

Nor did my father drive us to some ex-family-farm and stand in the driveway, as we kicked at the grass, tried to step on grasshoppers, or just sat in the van, our fingers pressed against the windows.

Until my grandparents moved here a few years ago, I had no personal memories of Missouri. No reason to visit the place.

Nonetheless, the thought troubles me. Why the North Shore? Why not Missouri?

And if Sawbill is an arbitrary location for my longing, what does that mean?

I push the thought away.

A few days later, we are back on the road. Because my grandpa has an early morning doctor's appointment, we do not stop and say goodbye. We pack our bags, eat the hotel's continental breakfast, and then drive north behind my aunt and uncle. When they pull off the highway for gas an hour into the trip, we wave at them and continue on.

"Think they'll stop at the farm?" my mom asks.

"Maybe," my dad says.

We take a northwestern route toward Kansas City then jut

northeast on I-35 toward Des Moines and eventually Minnesota. My dad insists on driving, even though my mom and I offer to help. I pull out the notebooks I have brought to use for my research. I had meant to ask my family questions about the North Shore, but I haven't. I had waited for my aunt to bring it up, for my grandma to mention the trip and say how she would love to see how it's changed.

Now, with the eleven-hour return trip ahead of us, I tell myself I will ask my parents about the North Shore. I hold the yellow legal pad in my lap, but still my reticence silences me. I do not know how to begin or what to ask in order to get the right answer, and so far, they haven't even decided if they'll come join me for part of the trip. Between my brother's arrival that weekend and my dad's upcoming business trip, my mom isn't sure they'll be able to squeeze it in.

I pick at the edge of the legal pad, which has begun to curl from the way I've stuffed it in my backpack. I snap and unsnap my pen. It feels like I'm giving them an opportunity—an excuse, even—yet the excuse to visit Grand Marais once more apparently isn't tempting enough to rearrange schedules, to block off a few days in the week. I clench my jaw, adjust my position, and move the seatbelt lower on my swelling abdomen as a wave of betrayal washes over me and then subsides.

Maybe I really am the only one who desires that location the way I do, I think. Maybe everyone else has moved on. For them, the North Shore is nothing more than the location of our childhood vacations. It's merely a fond memory—or not-so-fond memory, even, for my sister, Emily, who never did enjoy backpacking to begin with. Emily, who even on this trip to Missouri packed high heels and fashionable flats instead of sturdy walking sandals, like the rest of us.

I close the legal pad and open my journal. *What, really, am I looking for?* I write. The question sits there and quivers, waiting for an answer.

As we pass into Iowa, I close my journal. What attracts me to the North Shore, I realize, isn't just the red rocks, the pine trees, and the agates, but it's also the people: the five of us camping or skipping stones or holding our breath through the tunnels. Sitting here in the car, it suddenly feels strange—even wrong—for me to head up there alone.

The realization gives me the gumption to interview my family.

"So," I say, breaking the silence. "What's your favorite memory of the North Shore?"

"Oh," my mom says. "Trips to Duluth when you guys were young. Backpacking. Skipping rocks near the shore."

I nod, stare at the back of her head as she cocks it to the side. "What else?"

"What about you?" my mom responds instead, glancing backward.

The radio is loud enough that I must lean forward to hear my mother talk. What can I say? Everything?

"Backpacking. I always enjoyed our backpacking trips," I say. "And going through the tunnels. That, too."

"Will you hold your breath this time?" she asks.

"Maybe. We'll see," I say. I smile, turn to my sister, who has lowered her book into her lap. "And you, Em?"

She smirks and fingers a strand of hair she'd carefully straightened that morning, unlike me, who had just pulled it back, still wet from the shower. "Hotels and motels. The times we stayed in them."

"Really?"

She shrugs.

"You never enjoyed camping?"

"I preferred the hotels."

I frown. "Okay." I adjust my shoulders, stretch my back from side to side, and gaze at my dad's head, thinning near the crown now. I wait for him to speak, and when he doesn't, I inhale deeply through my nose. "And you, Dad?" I say, my knees tight against each other, my toes scrunched in my shoes.

"Sounds good," he answers, his hands on the wheel, his gaze ahead.

"This is for her book," my mom says. "You don't have anything else to say?"

My dad nods his head, much like I had just nodded mine. "What you all said sounds good," he says.

I scrunch my toes tighter and look outside the window at the cornfields and passing cars.

SOLBAKKEN

I LEAVE THE Twin Cities, en route to Solbakken, shortly after one o'clock on Sunday. It rains around Minneapolis, but the skies clear south of Duluth. I flip between radio stations as I drive, not entirely listening to any of the songs. My feet rest on the pedals, my hands on the wheel—occasionally reaching for the plastic bag of grapes on the seat beside me and then the smaller bag of peanut M&Ms.

Here's where Jeff used to have baseball tournaments, I think as I pass Forest Lake. And then, near Pine City, *Here's where we pulled off for lunch on our way to the MS TRAM*. RVs and trucks pulling boats crowd the interstate heading south, but the northern lanes move at a steady pace. I roll my shoulders, take deep breaths, push my lower back into the seat. I am stiff from all the driving these past few days, nervous about the week ahead. As the radio crackles, I hit the scan button, letting the antenna roll through the country and Christian stations that tend to abound in this area.

Just south of Duluth, the traffic thickens, slightly, as it always does. The interstate has been climbing for quite a few miles now, but an incline appears in the distance, the black fall of space behind it, light and misty as if I can already see Lake Superior. I stay in the right lane and search for the first rest stop, which overlooks the city. As the car crests the hill and Duluth appears, line after line of houses, hills, harbor, and bridges beneath, I pull off of the interstate, make my way past a few hotels and along the ridge. A small group of semis, a bus, and six cars dot the rest stop's parking lot. I stretch, breath in the cool air, air that rushes down my throat, into my lungs, where each ventricle quivers with a slight recognition.

This is the air I've remembered. This is the place I've dreamed of.

The rest stop's stone walls face the lake. A few children run along the expansive sidewalk, their coats open and flapping in the air. "Zip up!" a mother yells, holding her hat to her head with one hand.

I lean into the stone wall, into the overlook. The panorama catches my breath, larger than I had remembered. I can't even see downtown Duluth from here—just the beginnings of residential neighborhoods, the area where the lake narrows into the harbor and meets the St. Louis River. Beyond it: the bridge Kevin and I drove over a few years ago when we came into town from Wisconsin. Then the lift bridge we stood under for hours, listening to the thrum of cars above us, waiting for a boat to come, for the bridge to lift over our very heads.

And everywhere the water. Expansive. Not one color but thirty—pale and then darkening and then pale again as it meets the gray sky. A few barges have docked at the port. Another one sits miles out, hardly moving. Seagulls float and dive, and the wind—the wind. It whisks away the doubts I have had about this trip—my disappointment in coming alone.

This is right. I think. *This is right.*

And I am relieved, happy. I lean further into the wall, stretch to the left for a glimpse of downtown Duluth—the tall brick buildings, the line of hotels and boardwalks near Canal Park. *It's good for me to have come,* I think. *It was right to have come.*

As I get back into the car and advance through Duluth and then along highway 61, a giddiness causes me to turn the radio off, to crack the windows so that the air can come right in, wrap itself around my seatbelt, my belly, my hands. My family is everywhere. Pulling into Gooseberry Falls State Park. At Split Rock Lighthouse State Park, which has a new entrance now. At the highway overlook near Tettegouche, dropping sticks into the river, which foams from the falls like root beer floats, we say, and enters the lake in a burble of rocks and agates and stone. At each sign for the Superior Hiking Trail, I think, *we must have parked there once.* We must have driven up that road, or driven down it, or waited there for my dad to drive to the next access point and catch the shuttle back to meet us.

As the tunnels near, with their large openings and fat entrances, I gather my breath. The car darkens, but already I can see the sun on the other end. My chest hardly aches by the time I drive through. Tunnel after tunnel, each shorter than I remember, maybe because my dad isn't here, his foot on the brake.

I shrug off my disappointment. Who cares if they are shorter? I hold my breath at each nonetheless. I wish for a good week—for a successful trip. I wish that I will enjoy every memory and every scenic overlook. I drive, and my family joins me in the gray Chevy Lumina, our legs too short to touch the floorboards. We swing hiking-boot-clothed-feet back and forth, together and apart, smiling into the forest that surrounds us as we pass Two Harbors, with its signs for wild rice, as we pass Castle Danger and Silver Bay and then Tofte.

Seven miles later, I pull into Solbakken.

Solbakken Resort, which dismantled, reassembled, and then renovated Sawbill's original lodge, surprises me. I had assumed the resort would be hidden—tucked up in a hill or down a dirt road close to the shore, rustic and secluded like the old Sawbill Lodge. Instead, it sits fifty feet off the highway, hardly hidden in the trees. A single blue marker, rectangular and insignificant, announces the upcoming entrance. I must have driven past Solbakken many times before without noticing—without realizing what it was.

The lodge itself is squat, one of its "L"-shaped sides reaching toward the road, the other jutting to the right. The dark brown logs make it blend in with the trees, which crouch in on all sides. A string of eight or so motel rooms reach to the left of the building. Two motorcycles are parked in front of one unit, a van with a canoe in front of another. A woman leans up against a rusted car near the motel room farthest to the left and smokes a cigarette. She eyes me as I park near the lodge, and I wonder if she works here, if she's one of the owners, or if she's just visiting, like me.

I follow the signs to the check-in desk, situated in the middle of the "L." I pay the rest of my bill, receive the key to the "Telemark Suite," and am directed to park near the back of the lodge. A thin, gravel road circles the building. Rain has eroded sections of the road, and I bump and jiggle past the resort's lakeside cabins. The trees whisper in the wind. My feet sink into the damp gravel, coated with a thin layer of pine needles. I wheel my luggage along the plank path behind the lodge building and unlock my door.

I've made it. I drop my luggage and backpack on top of the small dining table to my left, next to the fireplace. On the other side of the room, a couch faces a coffee table. The back wall comprises the kitchenette, with a refrigerator, oven, microwave, and sink. Various, mismatched utensils hang from pegs above the stove, and wire shelving above the sink holds similarly mismatched plates, cups, and bowls. A wire basket beneath the sink contains an assortment of rags and hand towels along with a half-empty bottle of dish soap.

Behind the kitchenette's wall is the bedroom, containing the queen bed with its green, quilted comforter, a small desk, and two end tables. A plank shelf above the bed holds extra pillows and blankets. The room lacks windows and a door, not really a room of its own. But a cool breeze makes its way from the living room, carrying with it the sound of waves crashing against the shore some two hundred feet away.

I am here.

I lean against the armrest of the couch, pull the cuffs of my sweatshirt over my palms. The waves crash and the wind makes the trees sway, and in the weak light, the mismatched plates cast dim shadows against the pine walls. I close my eyes against a sudden headache. I rub my temples and reach for my Nalgene of water.

Across the room, the small kitchen table is set with three placemats. Kevin should be here. Or my parents. The doubts and disappointment that had lifted at the rest stop descend once more, settling into the carpet, into the cobwebs that cling to the corners of walls. I lean my elbow into the couch's armrest and brace my head. I grab my car keys from the table.

The Clearwater General Store in Tofte is more of a gas station than a grocery store. Still, it is the only grocery store around, and my family has stopped here many times over the course of my childhood. My father had been coming here even longer. Each day when my grandparents ran the resort, someone drove to the store for supplies, picking up flour, milk, coffee beans, and whatever else my grandparents had ordered. They parked in this very parking lot and picked up the supplies from the red shed behind the building. The shed remains. As my memory superimposes over my father's, I drive a stake into the ground.

Inside, the air smells faintly of fish. The linoleum is stained yellow in the center of the aisles. I analyze the boxes of cereal, the oatmeal, the loaves of bread and cartons of yogurt; everything costs more up here, where the grocery store caters primarily to tourists and only five hundred people live in the area through the winter. I pick up a tub of peanut butter, a small canister of honey, and a package of tortillas. I also grab three bananas—the least ripe of the overripe bunch—a block of cheese, a can of refried beans, a bag of carrots, a box of granola, and some milk.

Back at Solbakken, I unload the groceries into the fridge, stacking the nonperishables in a line on the counter. There's still half an hour or so of daylight, though the sun has started to slip beneath the hills to the west. I zip my fleece jacket to my chin and grab my camera. I loop the resort twice, walking in the ruts of the gravel road. On my second loop, I find a small path that leads down to the lakeshore. I make my way through the brush to the expanse of rock.

It is just as I remembered: the deep, reddish purple. The yellow and orange lichen. I meander along the small stones and large boulders, past pools of water tucked into rocky crevices, past small streams of runoff and heaps of driftwood, rotting now that they have floated ashore. Rock and pine jut into the lake on either side, forming inlets and isles, where sharp edges slice water, which laps against the rock regardless, a soft yet constant sound, sometimes spraying the largest rocks farthest from the shore.

A few ducks paddle past. A loon calls somewhere to the south. I climb atop a smooth boulder, run my hand over the lichen, press my fingers into the stone. I shiver as the darkness deepens. Soon, I should head inside. I have not brought a flashlight, and I do not want to stumble on my way back. But something keeps me here a few minutes longer, despite the cold air.

It's lovely, I think. Just lovely. And for a moment—the water hitting the rock, the two ducks adding their bubbly ripples to sounds in the air—a heaviness makes its way up my chest, so that I think—and almost wish—I might cry.

But I don't, and as the shadows deepen in the crevices of stone I just traversed, I stand up, stretch my legs, and begin the route back—back over the rock, the streams, the piles of brushwood, the glaze of lichen. Back up the slick path to the gravel road, to my small door, rusted at the bottom, and my empty, quiet living room.

The next day, I wake up early to interview Michael and Maureen, the current owners of the resort. Michael has told me he'll be at the front desk by 9:00 a.m., so I get out of bed at 7:00 a.m. in order to brainstorm interview questions. In the living room, I wrap a quilt around my shoulders. A mist obscures the shore, only revealing damp brush and the dark trunks of trees.

What I want is to understand Michael and Maureen's lives—to see how my family could have fit into this structure, how we would have acted in this setting if my grandparents had kept the resort and my family had somehow inherited it.

How long have you run the resort? I write down.

What first attracted you to the area?

What is an average day like?

What are your favorite and least favorite parts of the business?

I pause for a moment, dipping my spoon into the bowlful of granola.

History of Sawbill, I then write at the top of my notebook paper.

The white space of the paper dwarfs my five carefully written lines. I sigh, but I can't think of any other questions. Not the sorts of questions I can reasonably ask a couple of strangers. I put the cap on my pen, finish the granola, and take a shower. By 8:40 a.m. I am ready. At 8:55 a.m. I head up.

The log lounge is empty but large. A stone fireplace dominates the middle of the easternmost wall. Five feet wide, clear up to the ceiling, the fireplace boasts a grate large enough for me to stand in if I wanted. Wooden chairs and loveseats, with tree limbs and woodland animals carved into their legs, circle the fireplace. A coffee table sits in the middle of the semicircle, clear except for a few sheets of day-old newspaper. To the left of the semicircle is a white table with clean towels piled on one corner. To the right, a wooden bookcase stacked with board games and boxes of puzzles, everything looking slightly used and beat up on the corners but perhaps that much more welcoming as a result.

The northern wall faces the lake, though the trees are too full to allow much of a view. More carved chairs abut a five-foot by five-foot magazine rack stuffed with issues of *Outside*, *People*, and *Ski*, and old skis and snowshoes hang on the walls above.

To the left, another gathering of chairs and a plank coffee table circle a CD player that quietly emits classical music. The middle of the room contains an even larger plank table with a few armchairs around it. Today's newspaper is stacked in the middle, next to a dried ring from a coffee cup. Behind the table, the resort keeps a pot of coffee, hot water, and a basket of tea bags and granola bars available for guests.

I try to imagine my grandparents in this room, playing cribbage on a quiet day or cleaning up after the guests. I try to imagine my dad and his siblings putting together a puzzle in the corner. Their presence haunts me, not because I can sense them lurking in the shadows, my grandmother with a dust rag and my dad with a book, but because I know I am placing them here. I have dragged some sort of spirit into this room.

Michael and Maureen meet me at the front desk. Michael is thin, slightly balding, and his glasses and red-and-black-flannel jacket give him the air of a professorial outdoorsman. He is straightforward, abrupt and businesslike, and though he welcomes me, it is clear he has done interviews many times before. A single curious guest doesn't strike him as particularly notable.

Maureen stands behind Michael and greets me with a shake of the head. Her curly, shoulder-length hair surpasses my own family's wavy hair in its volume. She wears a necklace over a sweater and pair of jeans, and overall she looks more matronly than outdoorsy. As Michael leads us to the group of chairs near the CD player, she hangs back, letting him take the lead.

"So you want to know about Sawbill," Michael says. "Well, you might know about as much as we do. We've learned everything from newspaper articles and books. We know that Bill and Betty bought the lodge in 1980 and that it took them twelve years to move the structure. There's a plaque out front that says when they actually opened the lodge—1994, I think."

Maureen nods.

"Yes, 1994. They ended up raising the lodge by two log levels." He points to the walls around us. "So imagine this building with two logs less. That's how it was originally. Because of the added height, they had to install new doors, so the ones you see there aren't the original. Instead, they turned the original doors into tables. This," he says, pointing to the coffee table in front of us—a dark, heavy wood—"is one of them. Some of the chairs and the counter over there are also original to the structure."

"Hmm. That's really neat," I say, eyeing the table as I jot down notes in my notebook, my black pen moving in quick spurts across the paper. The ghostlike presences of my father and grandparents suddenly feel more real, knocking on the other side of the door-turned-table. I relax in my chair—a chair that very well could have been in the lodge when my grandparents ran it—and ask how long Michael and Maureen have run Solbakken.

"We bought it six years ago," Michael says. He raises an eyebrow and begins to smile. "At first we lived in the caretaker apartment just behind the check-in desk there. It was a tight squeeze. We have four children and it was only a two-bedroom apartment."

"Our king-sized bed filled the entire bedroom," Maureen adds.

"Yes, the entire bedroom," Michael repeats, shaking his head. "I don't know if you know this, but we also own Cascade Lodge just up the road. We bought that one in 2004. We were living in the Twin Cities then, I was working as an engineer and Maureen as an attorney. We were at the point in our lives where we were ready for a change. We owned a home in Two Harbors when Cascade went up for sale, and it seemed the right thing to do. When Solbakken went up for sale not too long after, we bought that one too and moved here. Solbakken is special. It has customers who've come through two to three owners, and it has an 80 percent repeat guest rate. People are loyal."

"How was the transition for your family, moving up here like that?"

"Well, Maureen can probably speak more to that."

Maureen nods, glances at Michael and then at me. "It was hard," she says. "A tough transition. It went okay for those that like the outdoors and the arts, but for those with different interests," she pauses, smiles and shrugs, "shopping, for instance, then it was more difficult. It's really a remote area. It doesn't seem like that in the summer, but it's a really remote area. There's not a lot of shopping unless you drive down to Duluth, and that's quite a ways some days."

"When we first moved up here, it was even more remote," Michael adds. "You couldn't get cell phone reception. There wasn't Internet service. It's tough for some teenagers."

Maureen speaks again, slowly this time, pausing between words and phrases. "Most kids who grow up around here want to leave after high school. They just want to get out. Some eventually come back but not all of them. There aren't a lot of career opportunities. At least not outside of tourism."

"The lack of broadband is a big issue," Michael says, his glasses giving his eyes an even more professorial look as he begins to speak quicker. "They're trying to bring it in now, maybe have it ready by the end of this summer, or at least next. It will really open the place up, like the highways did in the 1930s. Solbakken was one of the first to offer Internet service outside of Grand Marais, but our number-one complaint from guests is about Internet speed. It's too slow, they say."

"Really?" I say. "You'd think people would come up for the recreation, the views."

"That's what you'd think, but there are a lot of business people who just can't get away from work. Owners need to get into the twenty-first century. And everyone else—you have to strike a balance between the natural beauty and what you want to do with your time. But running a resort is like a small city. We have our own telephone service, our own TV service, our own septic system and water utilities. I didn't expect it to be like that at first. I'm really glad I have an engineering background," he says with a dry chuckle and a nod.

There's a pause in the conversation as I finish jotting notes, trying to catch up. I glance at the top of my sheet, where I'd written my four questions from the morning. "So what are your favorite and least favorite parts of running a resort?" I ask.

"The variety," Maureen says. "Every day brings new things to do, new people to meet. I like to be busy, and this certainly keeps me busy. That's also my least favorite part. You can never entirely get away because you're always thinking about things that need to be done. You work twice as hard in order to leave or take a vacation and twice as hard after in order to catch up." She mentions the two weddings they'd hosted this past weekend at Cascade. Both she and Michael had worked ten- to sixteen-hour days all weekend, yet here they are on Monday morning, meeting with me. I suddenly understand the weariness in her expression, the silence in her posture.

My grandma must have often felt the same—perhaps enlivened by the work and the steady array of tasks but wearied by their magnitude. No wonder my grandma sometimes only slept four hours a night. She was up past midnight finishing the day's tasks and then awake again by four or five in order to prepare breakfast. I'm not sure I would have lasted long with that schedule. No wonder one of her explanations for eventually selling the resort had to do with the work—how it just became too much.

Michael nods as Maureen speaks and then adds that he loves running his own business. "It surprised me," he says. "When we bought the resort, I wasn't thinking much about finances. I was thinking about tourism and what it would take to run a resort. But you really have to think about everything. We really got hit by the recession. Since then we've had to learn how to do everything better. Finding good, reliable staff was more difficult than I had imagined because it's so remote up here."

I glance at the windows, the trees, the lake, and the logs. What would it have been like to grow up in a building like this? For this to be so familiar you begin to lose sight of it, to take it for granted. If my grandparents had hung on to Sawbill, the specialness of those trips up north would have lessened, would have become ordinary. And if I worked at a resort like this, it might have become just that: work. I can't imagine anyone in my own family enjoying this kind of business—the management of staff, the constant requirements from guests. We are not a family of extroverts. Such tasks would have drained us. I shift in my chair, suddenly aware of the futility of my research. What an imposter I must be. Running Sawbill was never an option.

Maureen stares at her hands, clasped in her lap. I sense the interview wrapping up. Michael and Maureen have worked their way through most of my questions without many prompts from me, but one remains: what first attracted them to the area? As the sun moves higher in the sky, breaking every now and then through the thin clouds, I grasp at that question for one final connection.

"What drew you to this area?" I ask. "When did you first come up?"

Michael immediately softens, half smiles. He and Maureen stayed at Lutsen for their honeymoon, but he and his family visited ever since he was young. "My dad was a salesman, and I remember him calling ahead and telling Mom to get ready to drive north. I remember coming up to this area, laying on the warm hood of the car, and looking at the stars. I remember stopping at all the rivers and just running up trails to visit the falls."

"It sounds like me and my family, when we went camping up here," I say, brightening with the connection. "Like my husband and I, even. He didn't come up here until we got engaged. I wanted to show him the North Shore, and now I hope we'll keep coming back."

"It's magic," Michael adds as we all glance at the lakeshore, the gray horizon where water meets sky. "Every day I still look at the lake and am amazed."

REVISITING SAWBILL

LATER THAT MORNING, with Michael and Maureen's interview heavy in my mind, I pack a lunch, fill the car with gas, drive back to Tofte, and then turn right onto the Sawbill Trail, toward Sawbill Lake.

At first, the gravel road climbs slowly. An old logging road, it could fit three trucks side by side, and the gravel itself is so packed down that I find myself going fifty miles per hour without thought. Dust billows behind me as the road curves up the rumpled slopes of the Sawtooth Mountains. Every hundred feet or so, yellow butterflies clump over some small piece of road kill—a chipmunk, perhaps, or, as I continue to spot the clumps of yellow, maybe something less morbid: sweet residue from a tree or a flower blossom discarded by the wind. The butterflies, ten or more, hover over a single site, do not move as my fifty-mile-per-hour vehicle sprays toward them. I try to avoid the blotches of yellow, yet each time I pass, butterflies flutter in my rearview mirror. I wonder if I've killed any, but I do not slow down.

Ten miles up, the road begins to narrow, and with each mile after that, it thins even more. Now it only has room for two vehicles, and by the time I'm within a few miles of Sawbill Lake, there's only room for one and a half vehicles. When a truck approaches, we both ease onto the grassy shoulder.

Nevertheless, I drive with anticipation—with a need to get there fast. And although I keep asking myself what the speed limit is on gravel roads like this (surely not fifty . . . probably something more like thirty-five), something pushes me forward. I need to see Sawbill. I need to see what it is.

Once I reach the lake, I pull into a parking lot much larger than I had remembered. Half the size of a football field, the lot teams with cars, trucks, SUVs, and empty canoe trailers. Dust coats their undersides; pollen flecks their windshields.

Surely the parking lot has been renovated, I think. This isn't the parking lot I remember from when I was ten. I stall in the middle of an aisle before parking. I wonder if I'm in the right place.

My legs are stiff, clunky. My stomach rumbles, faintly queasy from the pregnancy. I walk back toward the road, toward the sign that points to the boat launch and the picnic area. A father and son pass me, returning to the parking lot. I wonder if they have finished their canoe trip or perhaps are just visiting for the day. Another group of visitors stands near the water, slowly filling their canoes with canvas portage bags and three large coolers. They wear long-sleeve shirts and khakis, bandannas tied around their heads. A dog barks while tied to a picnic table near the outhouse.

So many people. I do not remember it being this busy. I turn on to a slight trail and follow it until I come to a fishing pier a couple hundred feet away from the boat launch. There, I unpack my tortillas, my bottle of honey, and my jar of peanut butter. I slather the peanut butter onto one of the tortillas, squeeze out the honey, and take a thick, familiar bite. The wrap clings to the top of my mouth, as it always has. I lean into the fishing pier and eat the whole thing.

The lake, from here, is calm and narrow. Although brush obscures the boat launch, the chatter of final preparations wafts through the trees. Soon, the bandanna-wearing teenagers push off, zigzag a bit as they find their rhythm, and then paddle north until they become small dots. Another group pulls into the boat launch, this one a family with, by the sound of it, three fairly young kids. A dog barks, perhaps the same one that was tied to the picnic table. The sun comes out from behind a cloud, and I take off my sweatshirt, inhaling the scent of pine.

The bird I always hear up in this area calls out, *de dum, dum dum dum.* Beneath me, fist-sized fish shadow a lake bottom the color of rust.

The most interesting thing I heard from Michael and Maureen was about their children—how they struggled to adjust to the move. The one daughter had later chosen to go to school in New Orleans. "Most teenagers," Maureen had said, "want to get out of the area after they graduate. Some of them eventually come back but not all of them." Isolated and remote, without access to high-speed Internet, the North Shore didn't have a strong pull for many young adults, and those uninterested in tourism lacked career opportunities.

My dad would never have been able to live up here full-time. Not with his interest in computer science. I admire what he has done—his career in computer engineering and now as a professor of computer science. Yet that's a career he would not have been able to pursue living full-time at Sawbill Lodge. He would have had to live in Duluth, at the very least.

A deer walks up the path behind me. It pauses where the path splits into two—one route continues toward the boat launch, the other comes to this fishing pier. The deer stares at me, its eyes wet and large. The skin near its nose quivers. The deer shudders and bounds twenty feet into the alder, but then it stops again, as if startled to still find me on the bench. It flicks its tail every now and then before it finally moves on.

A gust of wind advances like a truck through the trees, filling the air with a mechanical roar. I stand up, pack my bag, and stretch my back. I walk to the fork in the path where the deer had stood and turn right, further into the forest. The lodge, I know, was south and west of the outfitters and the boat launch. Maureen said you could still see the foundations of some of the buildings. I walk slowly and search for crumbled rock. I want evidence. Proof. Some sort of gravestone. I meander around the lake, then away from it. Tree roots emerge like gnarled knuckles from the dirt. I step over them, careful not to trip. My boots sink into pine needles and birch leaves. Spiders spin webs from the damp limbs of trees.

I find nothing. Where is the grassy plain that the Argobusts saw when they first traveled here? Where are the molding carcasses of cabins that I swear I saw as a ten-year-old when we came here with my dad? Where are the artifacts—the fireplace pits and the rusted nails and the crumbling concrete?

I enter a small clearing, mowed down to create a turnaround for cars and trucks. Halfway down the grassy lane, a few empty campsites shoot off, marked by numbered pillars. Maybe the lodge stood here, and that's why there are no trees—why it's so easy to keep this part groomed. But I don't have a mental map of this area. I have no idea where the cabins stood in relation to the fishing pier and the creek and the boat launch. I have no idea how far the lodge was erected from the shore. Useless, this trek, without preparation. I need someone like my father to show me around.

I turn back toward the fishing pier. Again, I study the ground for the residue of buildings—for any clue that my family once walked these paths. I search slowly, methodically, but I don't expect much. Useless, I think again. How silly of me to have come, expecting the lodge to emerge. I return to the boat launch and up a groomed path to Sawbill Outfitters. A bell above the door rings as I step in. I want to ask someone if they know where the lodge once stood—where, in relation to these buildings, this road. But the two college-aged employees lean over the counter playing cribbage. They probably aren't even from this area, I think. I feign interest in the plastic packages of trail mix and screen-printed T-shirts. I do not stay long.

Back in the car, on the way down the Sawbill Trail toward Tofte, I drive slower than on the way up—thirty-five miles per hour now, instead of fifty. A black, weasel-like animal runs across the road, too quick for me to tell if it's a muskrat or a mink. I wonder what has happened to all the yellow butterflies. The road is bare. No road kill, even, to show where they once clustered.

As I near the lake, a fog rolls up the hills. I pull to the side of the road near a slight overlook. Fog obscures the valley here, thinning each layer of trees so that the hill in front of me materializes as if painted in five distinct shades of green—a very light green at the bottom, three increasingly darker stripes, and a deep hunter green at the top. Hawks circle in the distance. A mist chills my face and hands.

What was it I saw at Sawbill, when younger? I ask myself. Has the parking lot changed so much? Did we perhaps park in a different place when I was ten? Perhaps up that shady lane? The topography of my memory is so different from that packed gravel lot I saw today, the thin trail with no sign of an old cabin.

It is too early yet to return to the resort, so I park near Tofte's lakeshore and walk along the boardwalk—past a hotel and resort, kayaks pulled high on the pebbled beach, past the empty city park, with its empty gazebo and damp grills. I climb down the rocks and sit with my feet over the water. The waves come in, again and again, to slap against the black stone. The fog thickens. In front of me: blankness. A sound of moving water. A spray of cold air.

Sitting there, my feet overhanging the rock, the water a purl of ice, I realize I am not mad at my dad for not coming up here with me. I'm not even mad at him for failing to answer my questions with the enthusiasm I desire. I'm not even sure why I want that enthusiasm. Perhaps just an outward sign to show me he loves this place as much as I do? That he cherishes these memories as much as I do and wishes, in his own way, that we were all closer, centered in one place? I've expected too much.

The spray of the water and fog numbs my fingers. I clench them and cross my arms. The smells and sounds here are so familiar. Yet the people are changing. The resorts are changing. And maybe it's okay if no one here remembers my family. Maybe it's enough that my own memories are so rich and abundant—that each stretch of road brings another—that I can't distinguish between camping trips but, rather, they all blend together. How many times did we pass through Tofte and stop at the grocery store? How many times did we eat at the CoHo Café? My parents got engaged in this area. So did Kevin and I. At some point, Kevin and I will bring our children here. Perhaps what I've wanted all along is a shared love—and proof of that shared love.

These memories shaped me, and so I see myself in the trees and the roads, the mist on the shore, the lake water lapping against purple and red boulders, blackened with cold. I love who I am here, in my sandals and cap, my gray fleece that has somehow picked up an orange stain on the sleeve, my blue socks that are bleached on the soles. I am cool air and quilts. The smell of pine needles dampened by rain and by mist. I am the daughter who remembers stopping in a parking lot with her father—a man in a brown ranger's hat, a hand shading his eyes. A man who willingly traded his work suits for leather hiking sandals, zip-off hiking pants, and old T-shirts. A man who stared into the darkness, into the fire pit, into the sky and the lake and the fog and was happy there.

And perhaps that is the crux of it—the reason I cling to these memories now that my family has left, trading family camping trips for long-distance phone calls. Here, in this landscape, I am my father's daughter—most fully and in the only way I know how to be.

I do not rush to leave Solbakken on Tuesday morning. A mass of rain has moved into the area overnight, so I wake to a gentle mist. I lay in bed for over an hour, staring at the dim walls and listening to the footsteps above me before I get out of bed for breakfast.

I need to check out by eleven, and one of the Solbakken employees has agreed to talk to me about Sawbill when I do. Nonetheless, I am slow to shower—to pull on my jeans and sweatshirt again. Slow to wash the small assortment of dishes I have dirtied over the past day: a bowl, a plate, a frying pan from the quesadillas I'd made the night before, after I'd returned from Sawbill and ate alone.

Once the dishes are back in their places—stacked on the white wire shelves or hanging from hooks above the stove—I pack up my own clothes, zip my suitcase, and stand near the door that will lead outside to the car. I take one more loop through the rooms, touching the couch, the tabletop, the rumpled comforter, and the bathroom counter as I pass. I feel close to my family here, but I worry it is a closeness I have made up. A closeness I have imagined. What will happen when I shut the door behind me and turn in my set of keys? The room, suddenly, feels full of shadow—the metal grate on the fireplace cold to the touch. When my family left Sawbill, the rooms, too, must have retreated, as if even the skin cells my family had failed to wipe up with brooms and dust rags were already starting to disintegrate.

With an uneasy turn and an awareness of the inevitable, I open the sliding door, lock it behind me, and head up the flight of stairs to the lounge. Scott waits behind the front desk. "Ah, there you are," he says in greeting. Slightly older than my father but thinner and with a long, gray beard, he'd come up to the North Shore shortly after my grandparents sold the resort. He'd moved up there to find a job and to fish, and he'd stayed ever since, working at various resorts and renting various rooms around the county. Yesterday, when I was interviewing Michael and Maureen, he'd overheard us talking about Sawbill. "I went to Sawbill when it was still running," he'd told me. Last night he'd dug up a large brown scrapbook he'd kept on the resort. Today, it sits behind him on the counter, more than two feet by two feet, a worn-looking album nearly two inches thick.

"You're welcome to look through it," he tells me after I've turned in my keys. "Who were your grandparents again?"

"Chuck and Helen Case . . ." I watch for a glimmer of recognition in his eyes. "They ran it before the Sentys."

"Hmm. No, I've never heard of them. But I did visit often when the Sentry's ran the place. A friend and I would paddle in there. Once we even paddled in to attend a wedding."

"Really?" I say, trying to mask my disappointment that he did not recognize my grandparents. "That's neat. Do you know much about what happened after then? When it was sold and moved here?"

He nods, moves the scrapbook from the back counter to the counter I lean on. It smells of dust and age, of newspapers articles and cobwebs.

"It was supposed to be a two-year project, but it turned into a twelve-year project. The Blanks, who were running Solbakken at the time and bought the lodge building, had a set amount of time to take it off the lake. They numbered and dismantled the lodge and brought it to Solbakken's parking lot, where the crew hand-planed the logs since they'd gotten rather dark." He leans back, crosses his arms. He wears a flannel shirt, which, combined with the beard, makes him seem perfectly placed up here. "You can actually see the numbers they scratched into some of the logs to mark them," he says, walking around the counter and toward one of the walls, where the ends of the logs jut out, breaking the building into its two different wings. "See," he says, pointing up. "Around there."

I imagine marking the building, taking it apart, and then rebuilding, something like Lincoln Logs, though complicated by the size. Many of the logs are a foot thick, their grooves carved to only fit with the logs above and below them.

"The Blanks bought the building for $1,000, but expenses mounted as they moved it. The brakes failed on one of the logging trucks as it carted the logs down Caribou Trail. The truck rolled, breaking some of the logs. So not all of these are originals," he says, glancing around the room.

I cock my head. I've heard this before—the part about the brakes failing and some of the logs being damaged. I almost want to say my father mentioned that, but maybe it was my grandma, or maybe it was in one of the articles my grandma sent to me once she learned of my interest in the resort. The logs fit into place, one against the other, like the web of stories I've heard, though at least some of the stories finally agree.

"Once the logs were in the parking lot, the pace slowed," Scott says. "The Blanks ran out of funds, so they rebuilt as funds allowed. But it took a while. I still remember those logs stacked out there. They took up a good portion of the lot for quite a while."

Outside, rain begins to fall in earnest, quickly coating the windows. The near-empty parking lot grows dark so that we can hardly make out the road just a dozen yards past it.

Scott carries the scrapbook to the large laundry table near the fireplace. He turns on the small lamp in the corner of the table. "Enjoy," he says.

As Scott returns to the front desk, I open the scrapbook and discover it is stuffed with cutout newspaper articles and old photographs from the lodge's early years. The adhesive for some of the photographs has worn out, so they fall toward the middle of the scrapbook—black and white snapshots with dried yellow goo on the backs.

The first newspaper article interviews the Blanks, who purchased Sawbill Lodge for Solbakken. They had vacationed on the North Shore for years, and when they saw that Solbakken was for sale, they quit their jobs, moved to Lutsen, and became full-time resort operators. They, too, moved from the Twin Cities—much like Michael and Maureen, as well as my grandparents.

I turn the page to find an older newspaper article, this one describing a day in the life of a boat boy at Sawbill in the 1950s. Common tasks, the article says, included sweeping cabins, chopping wood, keeping the grounds clean, emptying the garbage, carrying water, and hustling baggage. In addition, the boat boys often had to scour the lodge wall logs, run errands, peel potatoes, swamp out boats, gas motors, and clean fish.

While a teenager, I'd worked as a volunteer dishwasher at a summer camp for a single week. The endless scraping of food scraps into the garbage and stacking of warm plates had drained me after only a few days. I woke up before the sun to set the tables for breakfast and only had half-hour breaks between meals until well after dinner. Though the other dishwashers and I had fun with soap suds and joked around with the cooks, I couldn't wait for the end of the week. What would it have been like to be a boat boy all summer? To be a boat boy for a family business, where the work is expected? I think of my father in that fish house, cleaning fish after fish for the visitors staying in cabins. No wonder he refused to clean fish when we were older.

I turn to the next page, where another yellowed newspaper

article describes Dick Raiken chasing a bear around Sawbill Lodge's parking lot. The bear was chasing his dog, Tucker, who was chasing a bear cub. Dick, the newspaper article says, hit the bear in the snout with a rake.

Next comes a series of black and white photographs of various guests from the 1950s. They sit in chairs and rest in canoes, holding strings of fish and grinning into the sun. Jean holds a gun with three men in baggy, khaki pants, her half smile thin and confident. Then she kneels in front of cocker spaniel puppies, her hands cupped around their ears. In a winter scene, she and Dick sit in Dick's workshop, making wooden bowls and furniture. In the dim light, their joy glows.

I flip forward, careful not to disturb the photographs or let them slide from their pages. In an article titled "Bears Rally Around the Garbage, Boys," from the *Minneapolis Star Tribune* on August 24, 1958, a black and white photograph—now more yellow than black and white—shows the Tofte dump my grandfather often described to me. Here, more cars than I expected rally around the pit, their drivers leaning against doors and hoods while a handful of black bears forage for food. In a smaller photograph beneath the short caption, a small boy feeds a bear directly from a syrup bottle.

This small bit of proof pleases me, as if it validates my grandfather's story. I pause at the page and tell myself that my grandfather and father once saw this dump. They were here after all. They knew the area well.

I flip forward more, hoping to find that the scrapbook proceeds chronologically and that I'll eventually come across some unlabeled photograph of my grandma or grandpa—some unlabeled photograph of my father, perhaps cleaning a fish. But the rest of the photographs are of Jean and Dick. Photograph after photograph charts their existence here—at the dock, in the lodge, in the woodcraft shop, in the parking lot. Various unnamed guests place an arm on Jean's shoulder while Jean smiles on in her loose pants and collared shirt, the top button unbuttoned. There are no images from the 1970s, when my grandparents ran the resort. Just a few more old articles: "Woman Guides Do Man's Work in North Woods" next to "The Woman Angler Must Prove Her Worth at a Fishing Camp"—a mocking how-to guide for women in the northwoods.

I wonder what kind of woman Jean was, and if these articles were placed in the scrapbook in jest. She must have been strong and opinionated. She must have been persistent. Jean overwhelms the scrapbook, and in doing so becomes the person I want to be— the person I want my grandma to have been. Jean has committed to this place, and for that I both admire and resent her.

In a photograph from 1947, Jean leans back on a trailer stacked with canoes. A string of twenty-three fish stretch horizontally above her head. At the left of the photograph, a thin man with a baseball cap and a dark button-up shirt leans against one of the trailer's beams. Two women squat in the middle of the photograph next to an old tire painted with the year. Their hair gleams white, their lips dark as if painted with lipstick. They pose carefully, their hands on their knees. But Jean looks relaxed, leaning back on the canoe as if she'd sat there before, her curly hair framing her slightly turned face, her feet crossed at the ankles. She knows what she is doing. She has orchestrated it all.

COOK COUNTY HISTORICAL SOCIETY

    AFTER SOLBAKKEN, I drive to Grand Marais in order to visit the Cook County Historical Society. The building, an old white church near the western side of town, stands past the main street with its restaurants and tourist shops, next to the donut store and near the Coast Guard headquarters, where walking paths lead out to Artist's Point, the lighthouse that marks one entrance to Grand Marais's harbor. With the Sawtooth Mountains in the background, the harbor's endless supply of skipping rocks, the high green cliffs of trees to the west, and the lake in front, Grand Marais has always seemed a quiet, quaint town to me. Other than Grand Portage, an hour or so further northeast, it marks the end of established development in this part of Minnesota.

Today, on this trip, Grand Marais feels even more like a last stop. I will head back to Binghamton in just a few days, and I haven't yet found the undeniable proof I've been seeking: proof that my family once ran the resort and that our name is in the archives. I want to know the truth about what happened to the resort—I seek deeds and contracts and old letters marked with my grandparents' signatures, maybe even a photograph or two, matching the photographs my grandma sent me. I will hold the material in my hands, this tangibility of my family's history here. Maybe Scott didn't remember my grandparents' name. Maybe Mary Alice Hansen only gave them two paragraphs in her book. But there we are: the dates and facts of our involvement at Sawbill forever encased between archival paper and handled with white gloves.

The next morning, when the historical society's director brings up the three folders I'd requested, each stuffed with old newspaper articles and letters, and a scrapbook similar in size and condition to the one I'd studied at Solbakken, I think I might, indeed, fulfill my quest. Within these stacks and articles, I may find what I'm looking for. I ready my notebook and my pen.

Yet the archives do not immediately provide any answers.

In fact, as rain patters against the back windows and tourists stream through the museum's historical displays, the archives at first complicate matters even more.

In a letter to the Cook County Historical Society from 2008, Sparrow Senty writes that she and her husband, Al, reopened the lodge in 1975, after it had been closed five years. Shortly after, I read a newspaper article that announces the sale of Sawbill Lodge to the Sentys in 1977. Not only do the dates conflict, but neither the Sentys nor the 1977 newspaper article mention my grandparents' last name. It is as if they didn't exist. I begin to wonder if there's any truth to the string of stories I've heard—back taxes and some tension with Jean—that forced my grandparents to leave.

As I read on, however, nuggets of information begin to emerge.

The 1977 newspaper article reports that, when the Sentys bought the lodge, the lease had been about to expire. "The lodge, as well as its fourteen cabins, docking facilities, and related outbuildings, have been up for sale for two years. While a number of parties expressed interest in buying it, most were scared away by the investment needed for repairs, and the $14,000 in back taxes," the article states. In order to address sanitary code violations, whoever purchased the lodge would have to spend an estimated $75,000 in repairs.

In fact, the Sentys' ability to purchase the lodge depended entirely on a complex agreement between the Forest Service, the Cook County Board, Grand Marais State Bank, and Frank Hansen, Jean's legal guardian. The county board abated half of the back taxes while the Forest Service renewed the twenty-year lease.

"The Forest Service went the extra mile in the matter," the newspaper article quotes Hansen as saying. "It was encouraging to see the spirit of all those involved. They wanted to see the lodge get back on the road and in operation again."

I pause to stare at the rain now streaming against the glass windows. According to my grandmother, my grandparents gave up the lodge because Jean hadn't paid the back taxes, as she'd agreed to, and the repairs for the code violations cost too much considering the Forest Service wouldn't promise to renew the lodge's lease. The expenses just didn't validate the work when my grandparents could have been thrown out of the Lodge by the Forest Service in three to five years, before recouping the costs.

Although I appreciate seeing these facts spelled out in black ink—$75,000 is a lot for repairs and $14,000 a steep debt in taxes—why didn't the county board and the Forest Service work together to keep my grandparents there? An inkling of jealousy stirs in my gut, and as I read on, it only intensifies.

Near the back of the manila folder on Sawbill Lodge, I unearth a newspaper article about the lodge's final auction in 1982. After reviewing the lodge's founding and describing Jean and Dick's decision to sell the lodge in 1961, the article provides a brief recap of all that happened after.

"Two more owners worked Sawbill Lodge after that time, the Lealis and the Cases. However, the resort was forced to close by the Forest Service because the septic and electrical systems were in poor condition. The resort was going downhill," the article states.

In 1977, the Sentys purchased the lodge and began making repairs. They opened three housekeeping cabins their second year and nine cabins their third. In 1980, all the cabins were finally "up and running."

They ran the lodge for two years (a shorter time, I am quick to note, than my grandparents), but in 1982, "the difficult decision was made to sell the resort to the U.S. government." The Senty's son, Mike, had married and found work elsewhere, and Al Senty, who was still working in Madison, Wisconsin, but hoped to retire in three years, couldn't justify continuing to work out of state without Mike as resident manager.

"The choice," Sparrow Senty said, "was between being able to retire in three years or to work eight to ten more years at the resort, plus giving up Madison friends and contacts. If we were 15 years younger, we would stay."

In the end, they, too, gave up the resort after only a few years.

However, the Sentys didn't back out quietly, and the resort didn't forget them as it had my grandparents. The newspaper's final comments contain the following quote from an "optimistic and long-time guest": "There is satisfaction in knowing Sawbill is finally closing down from an upbeat and active position. It would have been tragic to see it just come apart at the seams (which was happening before the Sentys came along). This way Sawbill is really going out in a blaze of glory."

The comment both irks and humbles me. Are they alluding to my grandparents? I flip through the last of the material, mindlessly taking notes on the rates the Argobusts charged guests back at the resort's beginning.

Then, with a quick dash of my pen, I draw a line beneath the notes and write *The Lealis and Smiths and Madejas receive very little attention, too*—as if that makes the jab at my grandparents, who apparently let the resort fall into disrepair, more easy to bear.

If my anger could be felt, it would heat the windowpanes, evaporating the condensation that has accumulated from the rain. I snap and unsnap my pen cap and frown at the newspaper articles spread on the plastic table in front of me. I dig in my backpack for a handful of nuts, which I pop into my mouth without tasting.

Then I take a deep breath and sigh, letting my anger slip to the floor, cold again like rocks on the shore and the water that laps against them.

Maybe my grandparents just weren't here long enough, I think. Not enough to really create ties with the community—ties that would encourage organizations like the county board and the Forest Service to help them out.

In an area as close-knit and rural as this, they would have been considered outsiders, and when they left because of the financial burden, any tentativeness at embracing them would have been validated. My grandparents wouldn't have shown the sort of devotion to place that would make them stick with it through the repairs and the uncertainty, though I can't necessarily blame them for that.

It wasn't Grand Marais or Tofte or Mary Alice Hansen or Jean that pushed them away. It was the cost of running the resort. Sawbill no longer provided a feasible livelihood, and so they left. As my family has done again and again, they moved when economics or quality of life made a new home, a new job, more appealing. Maybe they were sad to leave. Maybe just tired. But they packed their bags, swept the floors of spider webs, and drove back to the Twin Cities, just as I'd swept my apartment in Lincoln and moved to Binghamton, New York, and just as my parents, this summer, are cleaning the house in Mankato to move to Florida.

I slump in my chair. Without anyone in particular to blame, I have nowhere to transfer my anger, my dissatisfaction, at my family's nebulous tie to this place. It settles around me, heavy and amorphous, while outside it rains and rains and rains.

INTERVIEW WITH DAD

WHEN I CALL my mother the third day of my trip, she has news: my father has decided to come after all. My mother says she'll pack him a bag and pick him up from the airport Wednesday at noon to begin the drive up.

"That's great!" I say. "I'm glad to hear it." I hum while washing my face that night. I imagine skipping stones with them all.

But all of Wednesday, the rain that started Tuesday continues. From the back room overlooking the lake, where I spread out the thick folder of newspaper articles and old archives, rain obscures the shore, filling the windowpanes with a white mist.

My cell phone hasn't gotten reception since last night. I keep checking, wondering if my family has left yet, if my mother has successfully picked up my father, but the line at the top continues to read "no service."

The museum director isn't sure she'll get home. The road might have washed out, she says. An elderly couple announces that Duluth has flooded. The interstate is closed, and seals from the zoo ended up three blocks away from their pools.

Only the land lines work. Everyone's Internet service and cell phones are down.

"It happens all the time during a storm. They'll have everything back up soon," I hear someone say from the front of the museum.

I flip through the newspaper articles, take notes, and watch the rain. I wonder if my parents will make it—if they will even attempt the drive up. The isolation that Michael and Maureen had talked about claws at the windows with its white, misty fingers, and my stomach turns into a hollow stone.

I do not relax until after one in the afternoon, when the rain begins to let up and the pocket of my backpack, where I've put my phone, suddenly buzzes with three incoming text messages and two missed voicemails. They are all from my parents.

"Are you okay?"

"I've picked up your dad and am heading up."

"Call us when you get this."

I listen to the voicemails. In the first, my mother mentions the flood in Duluth and asks if we got a lot of rain in Grand Marais. "Jeff and I are just leaving Mankato. I'm not sure we'll be able to make it up to you, but we'll try. I'll call if we run into problems," she says, her voice tight, as if a rubber band is squeezing her vocal cords.

In the second, an hour and a half later, my dad says he has landed at the airport. "Your mom hasn't heard from you and is worried," he says. "I'm sure you're fine, but give one of us a call as soon as you get this."

I cut the message short and dial his number. The phone rings two times before my dad answers.

"We haven't had reception all morning, so I just got your messages," I say.

"We figured that," he answers.

"But I'm okay. And we haven't actually gotten a lot of rain here. It's been steady, but no flooding."

"Is that Jennie?" my mom asks in the background. "Oh good."

"Glad to hear that," my dad continues. "It didn't look like you were hit that bad on the radar. Duluth was, but it sounds like they've opened part of the interstate. We'll have a few detours, but we should be able to make it through."

"Good, I'm really glad to hear that. I'm looking forward to seeing you."

"Me too. We're about an hour south of Duluth right now. We'll let you know when we make it through. I expect we'll get into Grand Marais around four or four thirty."

"Sounds good. Drive safely!"

"We will."

When I hang up the phone, I relax the knotted wood that has become my shoulders. I smile, flip to a new page of notebook paper, and turn to the next newspaper article.

Late that afternoon, my family finally arrives. My father scuffs off stress as he always has, his shoulders and back relaxing like agates smoothed by Lake Superior's waves. He teases my mom as we stroll downtown for dinner, racing her to the boardwalk. He power walks, his arms in exaggerated angles, swishing back and forth as he marches past puddles, his legs straight so that they kick up bits of rain. He sticks out his tongue. "Ha ha," he says as my mom swats his shoulder.

Sailboats bob, anchored in the harbor. A yacht that had pulled in to wait out the rain now unties its moorings and begins the trek past the lighthouse.

"See, you could learn to sail up here," I say.

My father squints at the sailboats and nods. "Yes, I could," he answers.

"Wouldn't that be nice," my mom says. "Maybe we can buy a cabin up here eventually. Once we retire."

"Or Kevin and I could move here, and you could come and visit," I say.

"We could all come up here for Christmas," my mom says.

My dad smiles, sets a hand on my mom's shoulder.

"It sure is good to be back here again," my mom says.

Again, my dad nods. He rubs my mom's shoulder with his left hand and walks with the thumb of his right looped in his pocket.

My brother lags behind. He declined the sweatshirt my mom handed him as we left the cabin we're renting and now holds his elbows close to his sides. He is thinking about math, I know, calculating some equation in his head. "Aren't you glad to be here?" I ask. His eyes flick toward me, crinkling on the edges. He gives a brief nod, a short smile.

I turn forward again. This is where we are. This is where we are meant to be. Even though Emily had to stay home for work, the rightness of the moment settles around me.

We eat wild rice pizza at Sven and Ole's and then stop at the harbor to skip stones. We sift through the shore, searching for the smoothest, flattest ones. There are pictures of my brother and I doing the same thing when we were three and four in Duluth, our knees bent, our butts up, our pudgy fingers clutching small rocks. This time we squat, my brother's elbows close to his sides, my sweatshirt zipped up to my chin. I pull my arm across my body, whip my elbow and arm and wrist like a carnival ride. The stone sails, a faint glint in the darkening sky, and lands in the harbor with a single "plop."

"Terrible," my brother says. "Terrible."

"You should have seen me yesterday," I say. "I had a really good one yesterday."

"Sure."

"You just watch. All that pizza is going to weigh you down."

"I don't think so," he says. And sure enough, his stone shoots horizontally over the water, skipping at least eight times until I can no longer see it.

I shake my head.

I try again, a stone tight in my hand, but it quivers in the air as I release it, wobbling in its arc, landing, again, with a single plop.

"I swear. I had a really good one yesterday," I say.

"Sure," my brother answers.

My mom searches for a stone and joins us. She sets up her stance, pulls her arm across her body, and lets her hand whip toward the lake. Her stone skips four times before sinking into the dark water.

I shake my head in jest.

"It's okay," she teases while my brother grins.

The next morning, my dad insists we go to Java Moose for breakfast. During our family's last visit to Grand Marias, he had worked there with his computer while my mom, sister, and I had toured the town. Now, we order coffee and sit in what could very well be the same table. My dad's laptop case rests near his feet. "How has your trip been? Productive?" he asks.

"Yes, it has," I say. "I've gotten a lot of good information."

"Good. Good." He sips his coffee and takes a bite of his scone.

"It was neat to see Solbakken and the inside of the old lodge."

"I bet. Was most of the old furniture still there?"

"They said so, though the walls looked a lot lighter than in the pictures Grandma showed me."

My dad nods. Trucks and SUVs stream past the window.

"Do you remember much?" my mom asks.

"Some," my dad answers. He shakes his head and almost begins to chuckle. "By the end of the summer we had to eat Rice Krispies. Lots and lots of Rice Krispies. Grandma would stock up on breakfast items at the start of each season, and we were stuck with whatever was leftover. For some reason, that always meant Rice Krispies. I don't know why she always bought so much. But by September, October, we were eating Rice Krispies every morning for breakfast, sometimes with two spoonfuls of sugar. Your grandma would even crunch them up to make breading for fish and chicken." His right cheek lifts into a smile. "I haven't thought about that in a long time. When we bought Rice Krispies for you guys, when you were young, I couldn't bring myself to eat them."

"Really?" I say. My backpack sits at my feet, my legal pad and black notebook inside. But I am too enthralled to reach for them— as if that would break the spell, cause my father to stop talking. Instead, I hold my coffee just beneath my lips and listen.

He nods. "Let's see. What else? There were often bear around. They'd congregate by the town dump in Tofte. They wouldn't bother us much at the resort, but we had to be careful how we stored the trash. Every once in a while, a bear found its way into the dumpsters. But I remember one bear, a yearling. It was the start of the summer and really rainy. A miserable day. Mark and I were in one of the more remote cabins. I don't remember what we were doing. Suddenly we heard this pounding on the cabin window." My dad pauses, lifts his hands as if about to knock on some imaginary door. "We looked over, and it was the yearling, standing up on his back legs, pounding its front paws on the front window overlooking the creek. It was raining hard, and the bear was wet. Mosquitoes were circling its head. I swear it was saying, 'Let me in! Let me in!'"

My dad laughs, shakes his head, and so I laugh too.

"Were you excited to come up in the summers?" I ask.

My dad tilts his head. "I'm sure I was," he says. "Though I can't really remember it. The summer after eighth grade, we moved up there, expecting we were moving up there for good. I remember packing up the car with the expectation that we wouldn't return to Rosemount in the fall. But over that summer, the Forest Service changed some of its policies, and we just couldn't afford to keep the resort."

"So it didn't have to do with Grandpa's job? That's what the book on Sawbill said." I think of the conflicting reports I've heard—from the Sentys' letter, Mary Alice Hansen, the newspaper article.

"No. I mean that was part of it. Your grandma pretty much ran the resort alone. She'd head up there in the late spring, just before fishing season, and wouldn't return to Rosemount until after hunting season. But we really had moved up there that summer expecting that we were moving in for good. Your grandpa's job didn't change that. It was more finances. The resort had been empty when we first bought it and was in need of a lot of repairs. Most of the cabins weren't livable at first. We'd stay in a not-quite-livable cabin, fix it up, and once it was ready for guests, we'd move into another, not-quite-livable cabin. Eventually your grandma kept one cabin for herself, but Mark, Lori, and I kept moving around. It was a lot of work. A lot of expense Grandma and Grandpa hadn't counted on, especially with the change in policies.

"I did have a favorite cabin, though. There was this one, Brookside, I think it was called, built right by Sawbill Creek. The dining area actually was built over the creek, straddling it, so if you sat there, you could see the creek out of both windows and hear it gurgling below. Mark had a different favorite cabin, but that one was mine."

He takes another sip of coffee and looks out the window. The hills rise, dotted with residential streets and then just trees. Behind that: the gravel roads and the lakes, and somewhere south and to the west, Sawbill.

"Did you make it to Grand Marais often?"

"Not too often. This was where we went for any big shopping trips, but we primarily stopped at the store in Tofte and kept busy at the resort. I came up here much more afterwards, with you guys, when we started camping."

"Really?" my mom says. "I didn't know that."

My dad nods, slow and thoughtful. "Hmm. What else?" he says, looking into his coffee mug, his eyes slightly cloudy, glazed, a half smile playing across his lips.

For once I do not censor myself but ask the question I most want to ask. "Were you sad to leave? At the end of that summer?"

"I'm sure I was, but it was a long time ago now." He looks at me and then out the window. "It was a good place. It's too bad you never saw the whole thing."

A silence settles over us. The words my dad has spoken come to rest on the table, light as the mist that wets the rock by the lake. I breathe it in, hold my breath. And then it is done. My dad finishes the last of his coffee and jiggles the mug. "Time for a refill, and then back to work," he says.

I nod, still entranced by all he has said—all he has suddenly offered. In the side room of the café, the sun warms my chair through the window.

INTERVIEW WITH MARY ALICE

✽ AFTER HE TELLS me about Sawbill, my dad asks what I am going to do with the rest of the day. I sidestep, stutter.

"More work at the historical society?" he asks.

"No, I've finished up there." The sun burns through the fog so that shadows start to form beneath the cars parked in the parking lot. I can see farther and farther into the lake. "The director did give me Mary Alice Hansen's number. She lives in Grand Marias now. She said she'd probably be open to an interview, but I'm not sure."

"Why not?"

"Didn't she and Grandma not get along? I got that impression . . ."

"Oh, I don't know about that. They might not always have agreed on business topics, but she's a good person. I'm sure she'd love to talk to you."

The comment relieves me, surprises me. "Oh, okay," I say. "Maybe I will."

"You'll have to tell her hello from me."

"Ok. I will." I leave him in the coffee shop and walk back up the hill to the two-bedroom cabin we've rented. It is still cool enough to wear my zip-up fleece, but my armpits are damp from anxiety—the surprise of my father's sudden interview and the thought of talking to Mary Alice. For so long, I've thought of her as an antagonist, someone at the back of the story, pushing my grandparents out of it, refusing to allow them into the historical record. She was so proud of her own family's accomplishments at Sawbill Outfitters that she didn't have time for my family's. Surely she didn't like these outsiders. Surely, she made it difficult for them to feel welcome—to stay.

But everything I've learned since first reading her book in its entirety has told me the story is more complex than that. My grandparents, to some degree, are also responsible. They didn't love the place enough to last through the financial hassle and work. As I've gazed at those photographs of Jean and the newspaper articles about the Sentys, the knot of events and motivations that led my grandparents to leave the resort lost its mystery, hinting of injustice, and became just that: a knot. Facts laid bare, no life or sense of haunting.

Yet still, some part of me fears what Mary Alice might say. How quickly she could confirm what I've perhaps always feared: that we have no stake in this area, that we have no significant history at Sawbill. And if she does push us out of the story in such a way, it would be such an easy jump to say my family's camping trips and shared love of these rocks also had no meaning. Our togetherness meant nothing—my obsession, spurned by the loss of that childhood sense of "home," had significance only to me, in my head, which would turn Sawbill into nothing more than an empty desire for a sense of place.

It's a risk I'm wary of, which is why it takes me ten minutes to punch Mary Alice's phone number into my phone and another five minutes to actually call it. I sit at the small kitchen table in our rented cabin, the vinyl ripping at the corners to reveal the yellowed foam padding. I breathe deeply and bite my tongue. I fiddle with the cap of the pen, jot down a few questions at the top of the paper. *She probably won't even answer,* I think. My armpits grow even damper, my thighs tense. *You're being stupid,* I tell myself. It's now or never. I press my feet into the floor.

Mary Alice Hansen answers on the third ring and almost immediately invites me to stop by her house. She says she's not sure how much she'll be able to help—the lodge, when it sold, didn't make much of a difference to the outfitters, since by that point tourists sought canoe rentals rather than guides—but she'll try to answer any questions I have.

She gives me the address for a home less than half a mile from the cabin I'm staying at. I thank her and tell her I'll be right over. I pack my backpack, make sure my hair isn't too frizzy, and then drive the few blocks to her ranch-style home just to the southeast of town. She lives on the edge of Grand Marais, above the public campground. I glimpse Lake Superior through the trees.

"Welcome," she says when I knock on the door near her garage. "Come on in." She shuffles slightly, one hand resting atop the furniture as she leads me through a sparsely filled living room to her dining area, where four chairs surround a wood table. She has aged two decades since the photograph on the back of her Sawbill book, and now her hair is a thin silver. Her cat, Teva, butts against my calf, and I bend to pet her.

Mary Alice moved to Grand Marais permanently after handing over the outfitters to her children. Her husband, Frank, died a few years ago. Now, a "home helper" comes to assist with chores a few times a week. She asks if I'd like tea and moves slowly to the kitchen, where she fills the kettle with water and turns on the stovetop's back burner. She takes out two large mugs from the cupboard and places them on the counter. Her movements are languid, practiced. She must be in her late eighties, I realize; how odd for me to have held such a grudge. She is older than my grandmother, yet her house is similarly organized: the doily on the coffee table, the vacuum lines in the carpet, the one pet circling a chair. A clock ticks from the kitchen wall like a metronome.

As the teakettle heats, she lets Teva outside and talks about the weather. "The creeks that were dry are now full," she says, pointing to the trees that back up to her property, the creek I can't see that maneuvers behind the house. "But the rain is good. It was so dry last fall. We have to be prepared for fires more often now. Last year, we had to clear wood near the house—fifteen feet around each building. And in the fall, the fire by Ely got within six miles of the outfitters. The forest service recommended that everyone leave. They poured fifty thousand gallons of water around and on the buildings, but thankfully the fire stopped at Polly Lake."

The kettle begins to whistle. Mary Alice slowly makes her way back into the kitchen, where she pours water into each mug and carries them, one by one, back to the table.

"Everyone canoeing had to be hunted in," she continues. "But we couldn't find one couple for seven days. Planes flew over looking for them and didn't spot anything. The couple came wandering in a few days later—they had been at a remote campsite at the north end of the lake. They had figured they'd be fine even though they heard the helicopters." Mary Alice laughs. "They were peacefully camping, unwilling to think anything bad could happen." She jiggles the tea bag on its string as if it's a fishing line. "We even had smoke in Grand Marais. I swore it wasn't from the fire, but the deck was spotted with black ash and the rain didn't wash it away."

"Do you get out to the outfitters often?" I ask.

"Oh, I get out there once, maybe twice a year," she says,

smiling. "The home helper will sometimes drive me out, so I'm able to see the outdoors and walk around the campground."

"How has it changed?"

"It hasn't changed much since it was a family takeover, though they now use biomass instead of solar power electricity. They need quite a lot of electricity at the peak of the season." Mary Alice stops and begins to grin. "I read my book for the first time in a while—I couldn't stop reading!" She laughs quietly and then resumes. "Sawbill was probably up and running during yesterday's storm, since it has its own phone and electricity. It is kind of fun to be the one place that still has electricity. Winters were easier to cope with at Sawbill than Grand Marais since we had our own plow. Winters never bothered me. They're harder here, when it takes a while for the roads to get cleared. Sometimes I'm stuck inside for days."

"How have the winters been lately? I know ours was really mild."

"Yes, there wasn't much snow this past year. At Sawbill, sometimes the snow made high walls along the roads and paths. It wasn't like that there this year."

She pauses and we both take our tea bags from the mugs and set them on a small plate.

"Most people love the area—they fall in love. But some are frightened by the wilderness, unable to cope. I don't like to see people go out by themselves. It's challenging enough to go for a paddle by yourself. It makes me nervous, especially since most who take a solo trip go in spring and fall, when it's less busy. Once, a woman and her two kids went to Frost Lake and got stranded. She was a beautician from the Chicago area, I think. She somehow pulled herself together and canoed out to the Gunflint Trail. It was pretty scary while it lasted, but when they returned to the outfitters, the kids were bland about it. They showed no sign of admitting they ever were in trouble . . ." She shakes her head.

"I've never really been interested in solo trips," I say. "It's not the thing for me."

"Me either," she says. "And with two kids . . ." she shakes her head again.

"How do you like living in Grand Marais now?" I ask. "Do you ever miss living at the outfitters?"

"You know, I don't think about missing Sawbill at all. I'm happy to be here, embedded in community—and I have my little woods out back. Frank and I commuted for twenty years when we first started the outfitters and hardly visited Grand Marais. In 1976, when we made this our full-time residence, we began participating in the community. We quickly got involved in activities when we moved here full-time. It surprises me that I don't think about the people I left in the Twin Cities. I'm busy with being here." She chuckles, softly. "That's why I can't remember much about the sixties. What I remember most is commuting—those many trips from Bloomington to Sawbill. I can remember each part of the drive. So repetitious."

"Yes, I can imagine!" I say. "My grandparents did that for quite a while too—my grandfather even during the summer."

"It's amazing how many people commuted like that. To the Gunflint Trail, even. People came up here from all over, and the Gunflint is harder to get to."

I think about my grandparents, driving my dad and his siblings up to the Gunflint Trail from rural Iowa when my father was young. I think of all the Chicago tourists who drove to Sawbill at the resort's beginning and when my grandparents ran it.

"When we first came up here," Mary Alice continues, "I envisioned that other people lived here all their lives, but that's not true at all."

"No, it isn't," I agree, wide-eyed, surprised that we shared the same assumption. My energy rises as the sun glints through the window and Teva, outside, moves from one spot on the porch to another.

"Customers assumed this, too. When they came, they would explain where Minneapolis was. They saw me as being embedded here full-time. But I had lived in Bloomington! I could have been their neighbor."

I lean back with a sudden wave of tenderness and return Mary Alice's smile. We both take another sip of our tea.

"This is the first year that none of the next generation is working at the outfitters—no grandchildren. Just Bill and Cindy," Mary Alice says. "It's kind of sad, because we were hoping that someone would take over."

I nod, frown in empathy.

"Bill would like to think that someone will take over. He says he'll stay till he's in his seventies, which is fine with me—I don't want to know if it's torn down!" She holds her hands on top of the table, rubbing her fingers together. "My great-grandchildren are studying to be lawyers and pharmacists. They're studying media, computer science, and the medical field. Each has had a turn at being involved, but . . . times change." She laughs, slow and light, like the sunlight glimmering through half-pulled drapes in the window above the empty kitchen sink. "But I'm hoping that our professionals will retire and establish a new career," she pauses, looks out the window, "though they're not in occupations that lend to summers off, unfortunately."

A silence rests over the table, drifting between us. I stare out the window with her, at the line of trees near the back, at Teva, spread out in a patch of sun on the wooden deck. The woods cloak the backyard here so that, for all I know, we could be deep in the forest, in a cabin up at Sawbill. "Oh, look behind you slowly, a goldfinch," Mary Alice says, smiling, pointing to a yellow bird up in a tree. "What a pretty bird."

The goldfinch preens itself from the branch, just out of sight of the cat, who closes her eyes in the sun and lifts her nose to the air. Mary Alice adjusts her glasses on her nose; she is so much more serene in person than I had imagined based on her photograph in the back of her book and my endless conjuring. I am humbled by her love of this place, by her sad understanding of the outfitter's potential loss in the future. Her family, too, is changing, the place she'd built with her husband no longer a solid grounding for future generations. Perhaps when she thinks of it, she also sees the outfitters and Sawbill as a fleeting memory.

"I'm not sure this has been helpful," she says. "But I have enjoyed talking about Sawbill again."

"Oh, it has been very helpful," I say. "Very helpful." I take another sip of tea, swirl the remaining liquid around the bottom of the mug. When interviewing the owners of Solbakken, I'd suggested that Sawbill's history encompassed my curiosity—that I merely sought facts about my family's experience. Mary Alice's openness unhinges me, and for the first time I feel compelled to share more. "I'm actually really interested in movement," I say, softer this time, my head cocked. "My dad took my family camping up here a lot when I was younger, and since then I've always wished my grandparents had somehow hung on to Sawbill Lodge—that we had a reason to keep coming back, especially once my grandparents moved from Minnesota. I had assumed that most people who ran resorts and things like that up here were, I guess, emplaced in a way my family never was. And so it is really interesting—really helpful—to hear otherwise, if that makes sense."

"Yes, it does," she says.

"So learning about movement in general, what brings people to this area and what takes them away, is as helpful as anything else. It's fascinating to me, really."

"Where are your dad and his siblings now?"

"My parents have lived in Mankato for a while, but they're actually moving to Florida next month. Lindy, the oldest, still lives on Lake Mille Lacs. Mark, the next oldest, lived in Idaho for a long time but is now in Montana, and Lori, who was still quite young when my grandparents owned the resort, has also lived in Montana for a while."

"Lots of people from this area go to Montana, especially for college. It's a school for nature-loving people, I think. Two of my grandchildren are out there. It's kind of a tradition around here to go to school in Montana. And some of them come home, but some don't. Claire, one of my grandchildren, always told me that she'd come back—that she couldn't leave Lake Superior—but you'll go where you have to. It's the difficult thing about the tourism business. It's really hard to keep going in the winter. It doesn't bring in money or keep jobs."

"Yes, that's true," I say, quiet with reservation.

"Mike Senty is actually still in town though, building log cabins."

"Really?"

"Yes. If you drive up the road here, you'll see one. He gained a lot of experience transporting the lodge to Solbakken. He's made a career of it now. Frank and Jean Michaels were long-time customers from Rochester. They liked to fish during the day and party at night. Now they live in Duluth, though they're originally from Rochester. A lot of the people I used to know are gone now. That's what happens, I guess."

I sense the interview wrapping up. Mary Alice has begun to slump in her chair, and I fear I've worn her out. I finish the last, now cold, sip of tea from my mug. "Thank you so much for the tea and for talking with me. I've really enjoyed it," I say.

"Oh, it's been a pleasure. It's always nice to think about Sawbill again."

As I pack up my bag, Mary Alice lets Teva in from the porch. I take the two empty mugs and place them in the kitchen sink.

"You know," Mary Alice says, closing the sliding door behind her as the cat slinks back in, "the reason I can't remember much about your grandparents is that they were good, solid, everyday people, unlike some of the owners who were much more colorful. Yes. Good, solid, everyday people."

I smile and thank her. I wonder if she is lying—if perhaps she doesn't quite remember them at all, vision blurred by age—but the comment nonetheless appeases me. I am glad I came, glad I spoke with her. She is a person, like the rest of us, with her own experiences of place. How could I have resented her? As I leave Mary Alice's apartment, Lake Superior glints in the horizon, beyond her backyard, and for perhaps the first time, my longing for these waters, for a rooted life here, is softened by something like acceptance.

UNIDENTIFIABLE BIRD

🌿 IN NEARLY ALL of my memories of the North Shore, I hear a particular bird. I cannot name the bird, but its soft call functions like a thread, stitching together dozens of camping trips.

In the first memory, I am twelve. The sun slits through the tent around six in the morning. A heat I did not feel when I first awoke at three settles into the corners, sifting against the tarp. My sister stirs and then sighs. From the other tent across the campsite, my father snores. He will wake up soon, but right now it is just me. Me and these birds up in the trees. *De dum, dum dum dum, dum dum dum,* I think they sing. Or one of them sings. One bird I cannot name and then perhaps another farther off, returning the call from some other part of the forest—some other part of the state park. I have come to associate the call with the ash in the fire pit and the pebbles on the shore; with the coolness of the air and the games of Go Fish we play when it rains; meals rehydrated with boiling water and then eaten out of packages; blisters covered with moleskin. And always the *de dum, dum dum dum.*

"What is that bird?" I ask in the morning, once my father unzips his tent to boil water for oatmeal and I emerge as well, pulling a sweatshirt over my head as I stoop through the vestibule.

"Which bird?"

"The one that was singing earlier. *De dum, dum dum dum*, or something like that," my hum tentative, shaky, like the way I whistle—I, the only one in the family who cannot whistle—or, rather, cannot whistle more than three high-pitched notes that cause my mother to cover her ears. *De dum, dum dum dum*, I hum into the morning air, damp near the ground so that I can almost sense the dew rising as I walk toward the fire pit where my father squats in front of the propane stove, emptying a Nalgene of water into the pot.

"I'm not sure," he says, and I know I have failed to capture the bird. Failed to communicate that sound, my hum too quiet, too off-key, though I think the reference should be obvious—how many birds have that rhythm? That pitch?

Other birds wake and join the bird. Other calls enter the air as the water in the pot begins to boil and my father takes our mugs from his stuff sack, empties a packet of oatmeal into one for me. Mourning doves, perhaps, or sparrows—species I am familiar with—and then, there—the *de dum* again, like an extra beat of the heart, or a doorbell, the scamper to see who it is.

"There! That one!" I say. "What is that bird?"

My father cocks his head, listens, hands me my mug of instant oatmeal and a spoon. "I'm not sure," he says. "I didn't quite catch it."

Yet how can he mistake it? This bird that welcomes every camping trip we take so that I've begun to listen for it—to not ease into our trips until I first hear its note. I listen as we set up tents or unload the van in gravel parking lots. I listen as we sit on rocks on the North Shore, as we kayak on lakes, as we filter water from a stream, pumping the hand-held filter into our line of blue Nalgenes. I listen as we traverse the Superior Hiking Trail, bandanas tied around our heads, sweat on our backs, mud caking my calves because I cannot hike without one foot rubbing against a shin with each step.

I cock my head and close my eyes and lift a cheek to the sky, and always the bird arrives. Always I hear its call from somewhere in the trees, thin and pure as the water in the streams or the rocks we skip into Lake Superior. So consistent, it becomes a comfort to me: a sign that we have arrived, that everything is in place and as it should be.

More than ten years after those camping trips, Kevin and I drive to Binghamton to find an apartment. We stay at a local state park seven miles north of the city in order to save money—a plan that sounded good from Minnesota and Wisconsin but becomes less convenient when I arrive with a horrid head cold. I am queasy, exhausted, and too congested to drive the thirteen-hour stretch from Wisconsin to New York or even from apartment to apartment. My ears keep popping as we tour the crappy apartments that fill our first day—housing with broken ceiling fans, open refrigerator doors full of rotten food, holes in the floor and beat-up woodwork. I worry that my head will explode. At the campsite that evening, I half-heartedly push metal stakes into the ground while Kevin puts up the tent. I do not unroll my sleeping bag but lay, limp on the tent's floor, a hand over my eyes.

Nearby, a family holds a wedding in the park. Their laughter rolls through the dusk. As their celebrations extend into the night, their voices grate like saws against trees, waking me as I begin to fall asleep. Guests stumble toward their campsites near midnight. A six-year-old in the tent nearest us vomits three times. "Not again," his mother sighs as the son throws up just outside their tent door.

Near three in the morning, I take my sleeping bag and pillow to the car. I recline the passenger seat as far as I can and curl up against the window. Here, all the noises outside are muffled. A cool stuffiness comes out of the seats. I let myself relax and feel my body lighten, though even then I do not fall asleep. My vision lightens and turns white: I begin to float. I imagine myself hovering over the seat in the car, six inches from the cloth-covered ceiling. I jiggle my foot and open my eyes to find myself back on the seat, an ache in my spine. The hours continue. Owls hoot, and around five the morning birds begin to awake and call out.

De dum, dum dum dum, one sings. *De dum, dum dum dum.* And in the haze of my head cold, I recognize the sound for what it is—the bird I have always heard when camping in northern Minnesota. A bird whose species must thrive here, too, these thirteen hundred miles east, in wooded upstate New York.

Maybe this move won't be so bad, I think. Maybe we were meant to live here. I listen to the bird until my heartbeat slows and I finally fall asleep.

Throughout my childhood and early adulthood, I remember the bird at random moments. The bird becomes a sign of comfort, of those mornings in the tent, our legs stretching after the long drive to the North Shore. In college, Kevin and I sometimes hear it when we camp at state parks in southeastern Minnesota. "I love that bird," I tell him. "Do you know what it is?"

"Which bird?" he asks, and inevitably the bird falls silent, or he mistakes the bird for another one singing nearby—a robin, perhaps, or a chickadee. Something I could have identified myself.

On visits home during the holidays and summers, I flip through my brother's bird identification books, but they do not describe the sounds I remember. I cannot identify this bird from the colored maps of migration patterns or the detailed drawings of wings and beak shapes. "Do you know what bird sings like this: *de dum, dum*

dum dum?" I ask Jeff on Christmas, after he has moved to California for graduate school. He just raises an eyebrow.

"That doesn't sound like a bird," he says.

Once I move to Binghamton, I befriend a fellow graduate student who bird-watches on weekends. One afternoon, I ask him if he's heard my bird. I hum the call and we spend an hour listening to bird sounds on the Internet. "Does this sound like it?" he asks after each clip.

"No, not quite," I say.

The mourning dove comes closest—its call the right pitch if not the same sequence of sounds. I purse my lips. Maybe these recorded birdcalls are all about food, or some communication unrelated to whatever song welcomes me back to the woods when I camp. The website only plays a single song over and over, and it is obviously not the song I remember.

"What does it sound like again?" the graduate student asks.

"*De dum, dum dum dum,*" I say, reddening because I know I can't hum, and the song I try to hum is halfhearted and tentative, like the whine of a broken teakettle.

"Hmm," he says. We'll have to keep looking. Maybe another website. I'll try and find some more tonight."

"Oh, don't worry about it," I say. "I'm just curious, that's all."

That evening, I search for more websites on my own but again can't find the distinct noise I've heard. I close the browser and shrug. The websites just want me to order bird books or fifty-dollar anthologies of bird songs saved on CD. I think maybe the bird is meant to be a mystery. But at a dinner party a few months later, I bring the bird up again. A few graduate students and I are sitting around a friend's living room when a robin sings outside the window.

"That's an American robin!" the host says.

"Seriously? How do you know that?" someone asks.

"Look. I recorded them on my phone and had my friend

identify them," she says, playing us the sound recording she'd e-mailed to her friend.

Most of the group stares, silent.

"Maybe you shouldn't live alone anymore," another friend replies.

"No, but I took videos of them. And look, I did it with this one, too," she says, playing a clip of a cardinal.

The group continues to tease her about having too much time on her own—the way she must lay on her couch, her phone pointed at birds near the window. I find her curiosity perfectly natural. Why not learn the names of the birds you see every day?

"There's a bird I've always wanted to know the name of," I say. "I can't describe the sound for you, but if I capture it, maybe I'll have to have your friend listen."

"I'm sure he would," she says.

I think about where I'd need to go to record my bird. Perhaps just a nearby park. It could be done.

But I do not say this in front of the group. I smile as they joke about the recordings, the things we do to keep ourselves entertained when we live alone. I smile and wonder what they'd think of my own obsession—this one bird I carry with me like a tune I can't get out of my head, a tune so constant I've come to protect it, to find comfort in the repeating notes I imagine at night when trying to fall asleep and in the early mornings when I wake up thinking about isolation, distance from family, the ideal way to live.

Finally, on my research trip to Grand Marais—on what I figure will likely be my family's very last trip to the area—I hear the bird again. My parents, brother, and I are sitting in the living room of the cabin I have rented. My father works on his computer. My brother, mom, and I play a game of cards. The day has been rainy, and as evening falls, the breeze through the windows turns damp so that I long for bed and the weight of covers.

My father, lighthearted and relaxed despite the slow Internet speed, begins to play a series of mp3 files he has stored on his computer. "Canoe Country," he says as the small room fills with trickling water, violins, piano, and loons.

"Oh, turn that off," my mom says. "Those loons are giving me a headache."

My father laughs and turns it up instead. "Isn't this great? Isn't it relaxing?"

The loons pick up their song, sing more often, closer together, as if moving toward some sort of crescendo or climax.

My mother shakes her head, frowns. "Damn loons," she says, and my father laughs so hard the laptop jiggles on his thighs and he must hold it in place by grabbing the back with one hand.

"Wait!" I yell. "There it is!"

My parents grow silent, my father choking back a few final guffaws, as my bird emerges. That *de dum, dum dum dum* the same as ever, though a little shorter, maybe a *de dum, dum dum,* more than a *dum dum, dum dum dum.* But nonetheless the same bird I have heard all along for the past fifteen years.

I strain toward the window, the darkness of the night, where rain continues to fall. Surely the bird can't be out there. Surely it can't be perched close enough to us for me to hear this well. Though I've begun to embrace the bird's mystery—to let it remain a sonic welcome, a reminder of all I do not know about these woods, this environment, this world—the bird's sudden appearance invigorates me.

"What is it?" my mom asks.

"That bird!" I say. "What's that bird?"

"The one in the music?"

"The music?"

My dad nods. "Yes. It's in the song."

And so we listen, all of us leaning in, it seems, toward the computer, where sure enough the bird issues forth. My bird, now among the loons and the piano and trickle of water. My bird, part of "Canoe Country," where it has always belonged.

"Yes, that one. I've always loved that sound. What kind of bird is it?"

"I'm not sure," my father says. "I recognize it, but don't know the name."

"How long have you had this CD?"

"Oh, forever. Quite a long time."

"Huh. I've always wondered what bird made that sound . . ."

We listen a little longer, but then the loons come in again, and my mother complains, and my father laughs and turns the volume up, and my brother shuffles the cards and deals out another game. The song ends and switches to the next—more trickling water and, for five minutes, no loons, so that my mother thanks the lord. But I am thinking of the birds. How close they were. How real they felt to me, coming out of the computer, so that I still can't quite believe they weren't outside the window, somewhere in the trees. And how, for a moment there, we all listened to them together. We all heard the same sound.

Yet no one could name them. Not my brother, who ten years ago carried around a bird book on camping trips and spent afternoons staring through binoculars at the trees. Not my father, who I continue to think should know everything about this area, these forests and lakes.

So close, I think. *I was so close.* And like that, all my old longings return—for this part of the state, for my family's togetherness here, for the sonic notes of this particular bird—only this time, my longings spark, electrified. The freshness of the situation—the nearness of that knowledge—eclipses my disappointment.

Someone could have had the answer. I could have known.

INTERIMS

꧂ NEARLY TWO MONTHS after my research trip, I send my summer school students out on a writing marathon, to journal in short bursts from various locations on campus. I head outside, too, and stake out a picnic table overlooking the campus. When Kevin and I first moved to Binghamton, I used to sit out here during breaks from my schedule and watch the leaves turn. From this vantage point, the broad sweep of the valley reveals itself, various foothills dipping into residential neighborhoods. The sight had comforted me—had made me appreciate the beauty of this new place.

Today, though, the campus swells with construction workers remodeling a fountain and updating various utilities. The renovations started a year ago, but chain-link barricades still mar the center plaza, orange tape designates temporary sidewalks, and bright yellow signs point out detours to the science buildings down the hill. I pity the freshmen I am teaching. An eyesore has welcomed them this summer rather than the sweep of the valley, the comfort of hills.

As my students wander the campus in groups of three, I open

my own journal. Two years have passed since Kevin and I moved here—two years since we hung a map of the Boundary Waters on our apartment wall and I asked my grandmother to mail me photographs of Sawbill. Have I come to any realizations about "place"?

I think of Sawbill, and it is a longing—but one I recognize I will never fulfill. I am here, and Sawbill is there, and I do not know what places will become important to me in the future. I do not know where we will eventually settle and raise our family. Perhaps I have even consigned myself to that unknowingness. The uncertainty no longer turns in my gut, making the room spin, but instead solidifies into a fact I cannot change.

This summer I had my students read Scott Russell Sanders's "Homeplace" alongside Richard Ford's short essay "Must Be Going." I first taught those two essays in Nebraska three years ago, when my father had just moved to St. Croix and the tension between Sanders's promise to stay put and Ford's migratory lifestyle had seemed the most essential of life choices. Staying put, then, was something I could eventually *do*—a goal to accomplish in a few years.

This summer, the momentum in Sanders's essay again transfixed me. As I led my students in discussions of place and displacement, that small hope once more pushed its tendrils into the dark. I want to stay put—to know the land around me—to feel that, by being emplaced, I can help the environment and care for a particular location.

Yet I have not made that a priority. Two years ago, Kevin and I moved halfway across the country, to a city of hills and trees and flooded rivers. Two years ago, we packed our U-Haul with brown boxes of books, and two years from now, with my graduate program complete, we will likely do so again.

Yesterday, as I was fingering the small lot of baby clothes I'd picked up from neighborhood garage sales, I recalled the studies about movement and child development—how children develop best in stable environments, where they grow up in one place.

Is it wrong of us, I thought then, folding a newborn's sleeper, to have this child now, when we're living like this: a temporary home-place, no down payment in the bank for a house? How many times will we move during this child's first ten years of life?

I want to place Sanders alongside Ford and say, "This is good. This is how I should live." But I understand Ford's need for movement as much as I understand Sanders's argument for staying put, and though I yearn to imitate Sanders in my own life—to have a berry field in my backyard and an intimate familiarity with the kinds of clouds in the sky—I must accept that this is a knot I cannot untangle. So many factors influence movement. I cannot predict what is best for me or anyone else.

All I know is that this child will be born in Binghamton, and that fact will remain with her forever, just as I will always long for the pine and the birch of the North Shore—the lichen that paints the rock like a flame.

My second morning at Solbakken, I woke early and could not motivate myself to get out of bed. Even though I needed to check out by eleven, I crawled back under the covers, holding the blankets beneath my chin. If I listened carefully, I could hear the waves against the shore. Every once in a while, footsteps tread on the floorboards above me—likely from a guest in the lobby.

I turned to my back and set my hands on my lower abdomen. My uterus had grown large enough that it no longer hid beneath my pubic bone. I prodded the curved mass, letting my fingers feel out its edges, a few inches below my belly button and another few inches to each side. The mass was firm—a sudden manifestation of what was growing within. Every once in a while, it hardened, and the muscles clenched beneath my fingers.

I lay there for over thirty minutes, the blankets molding to my body, my uterus clenching and unclenching. The waves crashed, the clock ticked—lights slipping forward, from 8:00 a.m. to 8:12 to 8:20. People walked above me, their voices faint through the floorboards. A grandfather and his two grandchildren passed my living room window. I held my hand over the mass and embraced the quiet wonder of it. I didn't allow myself to think anything—to consider getting out of bed, putting on the same jeans and sweatshirt I had worn all weekend. I didn't let myself think about eating my granola and milk, packing my bags, driving to Grand Marais. I didn't even allow myself to think about the magnitude of that moment: that first trip to the North Shore in utero.

Instead, I listened. I felt. I acknowledged and waited through the ticks of the clock on the nightstand, the shifts of gears moving forward, my life moving forward toward a future I could not imagine if I tried. Layers beneath my skin, a tiny heart beat at 155 beats per minute.

How little control I have always had.

For four or so years in a row, my father took my family backpacking on the Superior Hiking Trail. We'd pack the car on Memorial Day weekend for a trip when the streams still stung of ice, and then we'd pack it again over the Fourth of July, where we'd plan our trips to end in Grand Marais, with its small-town parade and fireworks over the harbor. Those trips defined my summers, and even now they seem to stretch and groan, so that they did not cover four summers but rather decades of summers—my entire childhood among pine and birch bark, hiking boots caked with mud, rehydrated tiramisu scooped out of its crinkly bag.

At some point during those trips, I learned that my father had partly grown up in the area—my grandparents had run a resort. I clung to that knowledge, let it become something almost holy as I moved from one apartment to the next, one state to the next.

Painting walls, baking bread, making quilts, planting gardens—doing whatever I needed to make a home again and again and again.

And now a daughter is on her way, and I can't keep looking back at those photographs as if they define some set possibility that I can replicate in my life, as if I can lace my fingers around those ropes and they'll pull me back into some life that feels safe, if not predictable.

When my daughter is born, I will hold her in my arms and think back to that moment at Solbakken. She will sleep against my shoulder with her tiny eyebrows and a hint of goop in her not-yet-fully developed tear ducts. A tiny thread from my robe will stick to her lower lip. She will frown and burrow into my neck.

Sitting there—exhausted the way a new parent is exhausted, having slept a total of five hours in one-hour chunks—I will want this book to become what Sawbill cannot: a physical tie to me and our past.

I do not know where we will live when my daughter turns ten. I do not know what Sawbill will look like when she turns twenty—if the renovated lodge will still stand at Solbakken, if birch and pine will still grow around the lake, if she will have the chance to see it at all.

But she has come out of that experience. She is part of that family's story.

For now, that will have to be enough.

Kevin and I have moved the desk from the office to the dining area. We have cleared a spot among the bookshelves for a crib. We've even hung a bright wall hanging of child-like flowers where the map of Sawbill once held its honored spot, and we've moved the map into our bedroom. The map is frequently the first thing I see in the morning, and though I don't stare at it as often as I used to, I still stop there every now and then while getting dressed and study the brown section where Sawbill Lodge once stood.

Fourteen weeks pregnant, I lay in the fireside efficiency built into the lower level of the lodge my grandparents once ran. I lay there and listened to the waves along the North Shore—to the crash and purl, the crash and purl. I knew I needed to get up, to pack and conduct interviews and dig through archives. But I paused there, my hand on my belly, content, for a while at least, to make some sort of contact with that burgeoning future, that soft pulse.